The Story of Red Rum
and
Brian Fletcher

VICTOR GREEN

The Story of Red Rum
and
Brian Fletcher

PELHAM BOOKS

First published in Great Britain by Pelham Books Ltd
52 Bedford Square, London WC1B 3EF
1974

ISBN 0 7207 0800 1

Set and printed in Great Britain by
Tonbridge Printers Ltd, Peach Hall Works, Tonbridge, Kent
in Baskerville eleven on twelve point on paper supplied by
P. F. Bingham Ltd, and bound by Dorstel Press
Harlow

INTRODUCTION

Red Rum jumped the fourteenth fence in the Busby Handicap Chase at Catterick on March 6, 1972, just as perfectly as he had the previous thirteen, but David French, the leader, fell directly in front of him. There was no time for Red Rum to take evasive action and as he stumbled into David French he lost his footing and rolled over.

As Red Rum recovered from what to him was a unique experience and pulled himself to his feet, a brave young jockey was regaining consciousness in a Teesside hospital ten days after a crashing fall which had put his life at risk. To Brian Fletcher, the loss of memory was a palliative. With its return came the realisation that his career as a jockey was in jeopardy.

An accident such as that which befell Red Rum can impair confidence, just as a collision can render driving a nerve-racking experience for even a blameless motorist. He had always been a careful jumper but any fears that he might become too cautious were quickly dispelled. In 20 outings in steeplechases before the Catterick incident, he had not once made a mistake serious enough to put him on the ground; in 23 subsequent ones, including two Grand Nationals, he was to maintain that record so that when he went into temporary retirement at the end of the 1973–74 season his trainer could point to the fact that Red Rum had covered almost 150 miles in steeplechase races and jumped more than 800 fences and, that Catterick race apart, had never fallen.

Brian Fletcher's test of character was far more searching.

When he had recovered sufficiently to start thinking of the long haul back to fitness and race-riding, he left his County Durham farm to undergo examination by a London specialist thoroughly versed in riding injuries. His verdict was delivered with tact and was shattering nonetheless: 'You have had a nasty fall and I think you should call it a day and claim your insurance.'

That interview remains vividly clear in the memory of the jockey. 'I said, "I'm sorry, Sir, I wouldn't know what to do with myself and I would prefer to give it a bit more time and come back to see you in a couple of months."' The specialist granted him this suspension of sentence and so initiated this story of Red Rum and Brian Fletcher for, eight months after that desperate Teesside fall, the pair came together for the first time in a three-mile three-furlong chase at Ayr.

Red Rum, now trained on the Southport sands by Donald McCain, won by six lengths to record his fifth successive victory for his new trainer and owner. Henceforward he was to be ridden exclusively by Brian Fletcher and both were to make steeplechasing history.

CHAPTER ONE

Red Rum's Liverpool debut was made one day precisely before that of the man with whose name he was to be inextricably linked. Red Rum was a débutante in the Thursby Selling Plate on April 7, 1967, a race worth £266 to the winner; Brian Fletcher still was eligible to claim the 3 lb. allowance when he went out the next day to ride Red Alligator in the Grand National.

Brian could look forward with an optimism based on a sound foundation of experience to a bright future in racing; had Red Rum been able to project himself into the future he would, realistically, have seen a few years of undistinguished toil and, perhaps, a spell in a riding stable ahead. What else could be forecast for a cheaply-bought horse deprived of his masculinity as a yearling and hurried in his preparation for the racecourse so that he might fulfil the purpose for which he was bought: to win a selling race at the Grand National meeting?

On the credit side, his parents had stood up reasonably well to their racing. His dam, Mared, ran five times as a two-year-old in Ireland in 1961 and seven times the following season. There was not much of the precocious about her and though she reached a place once in her first season it was not until early August the next year that she achieved the victory sought by her owner and private trainer, Martyn McEnery. The event was a seven-furlong plate at Galway and her prize £202.

Later the same month she contested a minor nine-furlong event at Waterford and Tramore, worth £143 to the winner, and was beaten by 10 lengths. One more, unsuccessful, outing and then her routine was changed as she was prepared for a new life as a brood mare.

Red Rum was foaled when she was seven, the result of a mating with Quorum, a grey son of Vilmorin. Quorum had begun his career as a stallion at the Littleton Stud, Winchester, with a flourish siring the winners of 45 races to a value of £29,514 from his first three crops. At the time of his visit from Mared, his fee was £198. This was to leave Mared's owner precious little profit when he sent Red Rum to Goff's sale at nearby Dublin.

Quorum had been on the racecourse early as a two-year-old, finishing second over the sharp Thirsk five furlongs in the April of 1956. He made good progress during the year to earn a rating of 7 st. 13 lb. in the Free Handicap, the official assessment of the merit of the leading racehorses. Fifty seven two-year-olds were regarded by the senior Jockey Club handicapper as superior to Quorum, among them Pipe of Peace who was to be beaten by him in the Two Thousand Guineas the next year. Pipe of Peace's rating of 9 st. 5 lb. suggested that when the pair met he should pass the finishing line some 10 lengths ahead of Quorum, assuming that the meeting was over the Guineas distance of one mile.

Quorum made nonsense of those statistics, having shown already that his Middleham trainer, Col. Wilfred Lyde, had helped him to maintain the progress of his younger days. Three weeks before the Guineas, Quorum won the race for the Free Handicap by three lengths prompting the bookmakers to trim his price for the big race to 100 to 8. Pipe of Peace, the 100 to 30 favourite, was overtaken by him up the hill but a handsome chestnut called Crepello held his challenge by half a length.

Quorum went on to make all the running in the Jersey Stakes at Royal Ascot and to gain a narrow victory in the Sussex Stakes at Goodwood, an important race then as now but worth less than a fifth of its present-day value. Clearly he had more stamina than the great majority of the sons of Vilmorin, another grey whose five victories were gained over the minimum distance. Vilmorin injured a leg after winning the King's Stand Stakes at Royal Ascot and was retired to stud. The average winning distance of his progeny was just over six furlongs.

2

That of Vilmorin's sire, Gold Bridge, was less than five and a half furlongs. Gold Bridge, bred in France, won once and was placed in his native country as a two-year-old, scored three times both as a three-year-old and four-year-old, and his two wins as a five-year-old included one in the King's Stand Stakes. Quorum's extra stamina presumably came from his dam, Akimbo, by Bois Roussel who won the 1938 Derby on his only appearance in England. Bois Roussel, who did not run as a two-year-old, sired numerous fine stayers, including Migoli, Ridge Wood, Swallow Tail, Hindostan and Tehran.

Noble Star, the maternal great-grandsire of Quorum, was a very good stayer in the early '30s and won the Jockey Club Cup, the Cesarewitch, the Ascot Stakes and the Goodwood Stakes, all at distances of two miles or more. He also won as a two-year-old and his offspring showed more speed on the race-course than might have been expected from his record in long-distance events. In all they won 116 races over an average distance of 9.48 furlongs.

Quorum, then, could be looked upon as a stallion who had been moderately precocious in his racing days and one whose influence in terms of racing distance could be regarded as somewhat unpredictable though the sprinting line at the top of his pedigree seemed likely to put the emphasis on speed. The immediate impression from a glance at the pedigree of Red Rum's dam also is of a probable predominance of speed, for her sire, Magic Red, had a limit of six furlongs during his war-time racing duties.

However, Mared's dam, Quinta, was by the Great Yorkshire Stakes winner, Anwar, a half-brother to Tehran. Like Quorum, Mared does not have any dash of real quality in her pedigree nearer than her grandparents and in her case it was Batika, mother of Quinta, who was a mare of the late Aga Khan's breeding, being by Blenheim out of a mare by Buchan.

Buchan, foaled in 1916, was a dual Eclipse Stakes winner and also won the Doncaster Cup over 17 furlongs and the Ascot Gold Cup, though disqualified after the Ascot race. He was also beaten a neck in the Two Thousand Guineas and half a length in the Derby.

Quinta's attainments were unremarkable but her half-sister, Spring Offensive – sold as a foal during the Second World War for 100 guineas – had a fine winning record at a mile and a half to two miles and a half in Ireland and at stud foaled Faberge, later to achieve fame as the sire of Rheingold.

Thus the breeding of the bay colt who entered the Dublin sale-ring under the name, Mr M. J. McEnery, in the autumn of 1966 was not imposing enough to excite the interest of those looking for an animal with the potential to win good-class races, did not have any National Hunt connections likely to attract the buyer in search of a 'store' for chasing, and with Vilmorin and Magic Red close up on both sides suggested a possible quick return on purchase money in modest sprints.

Tim Molony, on the lookout for a yearling who could be prepared for a seller at the Grand National meeting the next spring, had a look at the colt and liked him. He knew the breeder well, having had previous yearlings from him, but knew very little about the dam's family and thought it unnecessary to delve deeply into its history.

His commission was explicit and when the lukewarm interest of all others round the ring expired as he made his bid of 400 guineas he considered his work well done. Mr Maurice Kingsley, a high successful Manchester owner, could be told that he had acquired a good-looking colt very cheaply and that he could now put his sights firmly on that Liverpool sprint.

Tim Molony had set up as a trainer at Wymondham, near Melton Mowbray in Leicestershire, after an outstandingly successful career as a National Hunt Jockey. He rode Hatton's Grace to victory in the 1951 Champion Hurdle and followed with a hat-trick on the great Sir Ken in the Cheltenham classic. He won the first of his five jockeys' championships in the 1948–49 season and the last in 1954–55. As a trainer, he turned his attention to flat racing but was denied the good horses which might have earned him the fame as a trainer to match that he so justly earned as a rider.

Today he values his memories of the two-year-old Red Rum very highly: 'I bought him to be a sharp two-year-old and to do the job he did,' he recalls. In common with the other four trainers who were to have charge of Red Rum, he was charmed by his temperament though not so charmed that he seriously considered keeping him as an entire. 'He was the most fantastic, gay animal; full of life and a real character,' he says with

4

characteristic Irish warmth. 'But he was a bit too gay as a colt and I had him gelded soon after I got him.'

That was in the October of 1967 when there was no Daktari-type drug with which to knock out a colt before the gelding operation. Nevertheless, it was performed perfectly and it was not long before Red Rum was showing his paces with other youngsters in the Molony string. He showed enough speed to make both trainer and owner feel more than pleased with their 400 guineas outlay and there was a deal of confidence behind him when he was led into the Liverpool parade ring before the Thursby Selling Plate at around a quarter to two on Friday April 7, 1967.

Blue Spider, a small filly who had been unplaced in a fair-class maiden race at Baldoyle the previous month, opened out as odds-on favourite and drifted to odds against as money came for Curlicue, a newcomer from the stable of Ginger Dennistoun, and for Red Rum who started as third favourite at five to one. Curlicue and Blue Spider got away faster than Red Rum and were clear of him with two furlongs to go. Blue Spider led approaching the furlong marker but soon afterwards reached the end of her tether and the race seemed to belong to Curlicue. The impression was deceptive. Red Rum, showing the courage which was to be his hallmark in his prime, had begun to realise what was expected of him and, increasing his pace, caught Curlicue on the line.

Tim Molony has a high regard for the ability of Paul Cook but, notwithstanding the fact that he had been riding a race-horse who had been having his first sight of a racecourse, was not impressed by him on this occasion. 'He gave him too much to do,' is his terse comment. His view that Red Rum should have won outright was not widely shared at the time and he had to go only to 300 guineas to retain him for Mr Kingsley at the auction. There was no bid at all for Curlicue, later to win a race of almost twice the value at Kempton Park.

Delighted that the bidding had been so light for Red Rum, Molony ran him next in a non-seller at Beverley and engaged Joe Sime, a top-class Northern jockey with a quiet sympathetic style. There were two other previous winners in the field and little money for Red Rum, whose price drifted out to ten to one. Once more, the pace was too hot for him in the early stages and though he lessened the gap between him and the leaders in the second half of the race Sime accepted inevitable defeat and Red Rum finished out of the first six.

The significance of Red Rum's performance was not lost on Tim Molony. Despite the emphasis on sprinting in his gelding's pedigree, he realised that five furlongs was too short a distance for him. Two months went by and then Red Rum was taken to Teesside for a six-furlong maiden plate. He had put on weight and condition since Beverley but the class of opposition was regarded as too formidable for him. A hundred to seven was freely available and those who accepted those odds quickly knew that they had lost their money. Both he and the favourite, Rising Water, missed the break and at the post only two of the eleven runners were behind him.

At this point in his career, Red Rum appeared to be well on the way to total obscurity. The Liverpool seller, it seemed, would represent the apex of his achievements. Here was yet another two-year-old whose only chance of earning his keep had been to trade on superior fitness in the early weeks of the season. Consequently, when he was sent North again to contest the Angerton Stakes at Newcastle and take on two previous winners he was at 33 to one. George Cadwaladr, a talented and consistently effective young jockey, was Red Rum's partner this time and he was to be surprised by his mount's display.

This time, he showed enough speed to hold a good position from the start and he was still in with a chance at the distance. Mount Athos, one of the two with winning form and later to run third in the Derby, came through quickly on the outside to sweep past him inside the final furlong and Waggy, another earlier winner, also caught and passed him, but he held on to third place, beaten only a length and the same. It was far and away his best performance. The ground was good to firm and it was firm when he next turned out, in a seven-furlong nursery at Warwick in late August.

Drawn number fourteen of fourteen on a course which favours the low numbers, Red Rum again got away to a good start and was a close third with two and a half furlongs to go. At six furlongs he probably would have been beaten by the second favourite, Rose Diana, but he wore her down in the seventh and ran his race out gamely to hold off the challenge of Parliamo by a neck. The first prize was £467 and the field one of modest talent, for Parliamo had not attracted a bid after winning a seller at Ayr the previous month and was conceding 1 lb. to Red Rum.

Still, Red Rum was proving to be a very game horse and a sound one, and most owners ask no more of their horses than that provided a little ability is thrown in, too.

Red Rum was to have three more outings that season. He ran reasonably well, carrying a 10 lb. penalty, in the Bishopthorpe Nursery at York to finish eighth of eighteen to Aniseed, stylishly ridden by a 5 lb.-claiming apprentice called Tony Murray; and then tackled the Pontefract mile – the stiffest in the country. Lester Piggott, well on the way to his fourth championship, had the mount on him that September day but even the champion could not get him near enough to the leaders as they galloped up the stamina-sapping hill towards the short straight. Red Rum did make up three places in the last two furlongs to get third place but was never a danger to the favourite, Stardao, runner-up in the York nursery. For his final race, a one-mile nursery at Leicester, Red Rum was fitted with blinkers which were intended to counteract supposed laziness. He did keep in better touch with the leaders this time but even some of the severest pressure he had encountered could not bring a response powerful enough to enable him to hold his place and he passed the post a well-beaten fourth.

Thus he went into the winter of 1967 as a two-year-old who had lived up to the modest expectations held for him as a yearling. He was never going to be much more than a selling plater, for sure, but he could be prepared for another early seller the next season and could win much more than the cost of his keep for his owner because he was unlikely to start at a very short price whatever the company.

CHAPTER TWO

For Brian Fletcher, the season which ended in 1967 was both a thrilling and a disappointing one: he had his first ride in the Grand National and more than trebled his previous highest total of winners. He was winning the battle to establish himself as a National Hunt jockey even if he felt that what had been probably the chance of a lifetime to win the National had been lost.

His entry into racing proper was unconventional. Not for him an apprenticeship to a good stable before increasing weight forced attention to be turned to jumping. Brian served a harder and more rigorous apprenticeship while still a pupil of Barnard Castle Grammar School, knowingly sacrificing his school studies for a hard education on the flapping tracks of Great Britain.

In the early '60s, flapping meetings – race meetings held outside the jursidiction of the Jockey Club and outlawed by it – attracted big crowds and big money at centres throughout England, Scotland and Wales: at Edinburgh, Appleby in Cumberland, Hawick, and many more. All had one thing in common. The circuits were tight and, as Brian recalls, 'on the bend all the way'.

There were young riders and the not so young, and youth it was who generally carried the day. When a dozen or more thoroughbreds gallop flat out to a tight bend, when the nature of the track is such that inevitably some are going to be bumped or carried wide, when it is not unusual for horse and jockey to go down amid the wild flurry of hooves, there is no place for caution. Skill and riding ability do count, of course, but a devil-may-care attitude to danger is of great significance and this fades with the passing of the teenage years.

Brian Fletcher was one of the top boys. He was confident in his own ability and knew that when the pressure was on it would be the other fellow who would chicken out, not him. 'This was the advantage of youth: you feared nothing.' The winners came in scores, hat-tricks were frequent, and all the time he dreamed of becoming a recognised jockey when his school days were over.

Riding was second nature to him. 'Ever since I can remember, my father had horses and ponies. I used to ride to the village shop for the groceries rather than use my bicycle, and I broke ponies when I was very young.'

Home was a farm at Cockfield in County Durham, not far from the beautiful and historic town of Barnard Castle. He loved the countryside and the warm-hearted people who inhabited it, and has resolutely resisted all temptations to move away from the area. He got on well at the village school and, despite spending far more time on his riding than on his school-work, passed for Barnard Castle Grammar School. He was still a pupil there, and almost 17, when Denys Smith called at his father's farm to buy some cattle.

Denys had just started out as a National Hunt trainer, having previously shared Brian's interest in flapping. 'I asked him if he would give me a job, which he did. That was the start of it all,' says Brian. So it was goodbye to flapping and all the perils entailed. Already, he was no stranger to concussion and he had experienced one fall which remains one of the most serious he ever has had. Tearing into a bend, his mount was knocked over and Brian's leg became entangled in a stirrup iron. He was dragged along by his foot and his leg broke under the strain. The bone mended quickly and his nerve suffered not at all, so although he had never jumped a fence when he joined the Denys Smith stable he was prepared mentally for the hazards which lay ahead.

The 1964–65 season was his first with Denys Smith, who had set up near to the winner-producing factory of Arthur Stephenson at Bishop Auckland. Denys's practice then, as in future years, was to book the best riders available while giving opportunities also to claiming riders attached to his own stable. Terry Biddlecombe had walked away with the championship the season before with a remarkable 114 winners from 531 rides and he made regular journeys North to partner the Smith horses. Brian watched him closely and listened to what he had to say. He formed the firm impression that Terry was as good a National Hunt jockey as it was possible to be. That impression grew into a conviction which has never wavered.

Denys Smith made an immediate impact on the jumping world and turned out winners with a regularity which stamped him as an outstandingly capable trainer: Usario, a novice hurdler, won five times in succession for him that season; Fortune Hunter, another hurdler, won three of his first four races and Terry rode both of them to victory on the same day at Wetherby. Brian had just over 20 rides that season and one of his three victories was achieved on Senior Warden in a division of a novice hurdle at Hexham in Northumberland.

Stan Hayhurst, one of his senior professionals, partnered a stable-companion in the same race. He was third favourite but finished out of the first four and his name was Red Alligator. Two seasons later he was to give Brian his first taste of Aintree and three seasons later his first great moment as a steeplechase jockey.

In his second year, Brian was given double the number of rides he had had in his first, and four of them were successful. Then came his third season. His right to claim the 7 lb. allowance disappeared when he scored on a 100 to 7 shot, Wor Geordie, at Newcastle in November and three months later, at Catterick, he was given the ride on Red Alligator for the first time. This eight-year-old had tried to run out with Pat Buckley twice in his previous race and, with Brian able to claim only 2 lb. of his 5 lb. allowance, he was at ten to one for the Grand National Trial. Brian sent him to the front with just under half a mile to go and he stayed on well to win the three-and-a-half mile event by three lengths.

Denys Smith was well pleased and let Brian partner Red Alligator again in the Durham National, run over the same distance and over the small Sedgefield fences. Brian's allowance was down to 3 lb. by then.

His seven opponents had little to recommend them and Red Alligator started an odds-on favourite. Once again, the young Fletcher showed a good understanding of the horse and kept him going strongly up the stiff hill to the line to win by four lengths. He was one of the 20 on bottom weight at Aintree and Denys Smith decided to let Brian have the ride again. This was a real tribute to his temperament as well as his capabilities for he was a jockey of limited experience over jumps who still had the right to claim the 3 lb. allowance in less-important races. He had been to Aintree as a stable-boy but had never ridden over the fences before he set out that Saturday afternoon on Red Alligator.

As preparation for the race, he walked the course beforehand with his trainer, who also saddled Greek Scholar for Terry Biddlecombe. 'In Denys's opinion, as in mine, Terry was the greatest steeplechase jockey of them all and Denys told me to try to note where Terry was in the race and run a line through him,' Brian recalls.

'Terry's advice was to stick to the middle to the outside of the fences on the first circuit to try to avoid trouble. The drops are a wee bit less severe there than on the inside at Becher's and Valentine's. When we reached halfway, and if my horse was still going well, I should keep in the back of my mind the fact that there was still a long way to go and so I should not begin to get anxious; I must give my horse every chance of getting the trip.'

Greek Scholar was at 20 to 1, Red Alligator at 30 to 1 and the clear favourite was Honey End. So often on National day, the public takes a fancy to one particular horse, forcing its price down to an unrealistic level. So it was that Honey End, the mount of Josh Gifford, had his odds cut from 100 to 8 to 15 to 2. Among the 100 to 1 outsiders was a nine-year-old who only seven days earlier had been a bad last of six at Leicester, who was having his sixteenth race of the season and whose chance was thought so little of that his trainer was at Worcester to ride in a novices' hurdle, and his owner at home watching the race on television. His name was Foinavon. It should have been prefixed by lucky.

Brian Fletcher began to feel the tension of the occasion on the Saturday morning before the National. It was a tension far removed from nervousness and it was increased by the long preliminaries in the afternoon: the parade in front of the old but distinguished stands, the canter back towards the first fence, the delay while girths were checked and the runners were brought into line. 'I didn't like the preliminaries then and I never will,' he says now.

But it was the day he had waited for all his life and he was ready for it. Red Alligator did not get agitated in the parade and he got away well towards the outside of the huge field. His list of opponents was denuded by three at the very first fence, the well-fancied Bassnet, and two 66 to 1 chances, Meon Valley and Popham Down. It was Popham Down who was to make the 1967 National go down in history in the same category as the 1928 event in which Easter Hero became stuck on the top of the Canal Turn and decimated the field.

As the runners galloped over the Melling Road and down towards Becher's for the first time, Brian was following his trainer's advice and keeping Greek Scholar in the corner of his eye.

Penvulgo was in the lead, from Princeful and Rutherfords. Also well there were Kirtle-Lad, Lucky Domino and Castle Falls, Greek Scholar was well placed just behind the leaders and Red Alligator was tucked in behind him. Anglo, the Liverpool hero of the year before and half-brother to Red Alligator, already was tailed off, and Bobby Beasley was to call it a day on him before the Chair.

Red Alligator lost several places on the long run from the Canal Turn to the stands but Brian was delighted by the way in which he was jumping and, as they took the water and set out on the final circuit, he could feel hope rising within him. An astonishing 35 horses were still standing and Red Alligator was twenty-first, twelve behind Greek Scholar but in close enough touch to the leaders, Kirtle-Lad, Castle Falls, Princeful and Rutherfords. Away at the back were Forecastle, Aerial III, the mount of a 68-year-old American grandfather, Tim Durant, and Foinavon.

Only five more of the runners departed either before or at Becher's the second time round. Foinavon, by that time almost tailed off, blundered at Becher's and his blinkered head almost hit the ground. His rider, John Buckingham, had no thoughts other than of trying to complete the course as the 30 survivors galloped towards the twenty-third fence, at four-feet high the smallest on the course.

Red Alligator had been eased forward and, according to plan, was closer to the inside than he had been on the first circuit. Terry Biddlecombe had tacked over Greek Scholar towards the inside rail and both were poised to challenge the leaders, who now included Rondetto, Different Class – going particularly well – Kapeno and The Fossa. Out in front was the riderless Popham Down. He had cleared Becher's but, perhaps fearing another jump of such frightening proportions, pulled up as he went for the inside corner of the twenty-third and then proceeded to trot along its full length.

As he did so, he went straight in front of the leaders. They came to an abrupt halt and Paddy Broderick, rider of Kirtle-Lad, Roy Edwards on Princeful, and Stan Mellor on The Fossa landed over the fence without their partners. The same fate befell John Lawrence, who had been hopeful of reaching a place on Norther, and Pat Buckley, also in the leading bunch on Limeking. Brian tried to find a way through the chaos and was knocked clean out of the saddle before he could get to the fence. Norther, who had to jump a prostrate horse, had landed in the fence, as had Limeking, and the horses following found their way virtually barred.

John Buckingham, at the age of 26 having his first ride in a Grand National, had more time than most to take stock of the situation for he was almost a hundred yards behind. As John Lawrence pointed out in Horse and Hound, Buckingham already had given one striking example of quick thinking when the only one of ten jockeys to choose the correct of two alternative fences at Market Rasen the previous season. He had been awarded the race on an objection.

This time, Buckingham spotted a chink in the armour in front of him in the outside corner of what is one of the narrowest fences. Foinavon squeezed past the riderless, fallen and bemused horses, dodged round perplexed jockeys, and got over at the first attempt. Then away he went on his own, for not one of the other 29 horses who had been on their feet after the second Becher's was not brought to a halt in the chaos caused by Popham Down.

Kirtle-Lad was the first to go in pursuit, but he pulled up

lame two fences later. Then came the plodding Quintin Bay, Packed Home, a 12-year-old who had been just in front of Foinavon at the twenty-third, Aussie, another who had been at the back, and Greek Scholar. Meanwhile, Brian was having three attempts to get Red Alligator through the still considerable chaos.

'If I had jumped the fence at the first attempt, after re-mounting, undoubtedly I would have caught Foinavon,' he states. 'But I was baulked twice. There were jockeys and loose horses everywhere. We all knew that something had come from a long way back and jumped the fence at the first attempt, which made everyone more anxious than ever. It was virtually impossible for a long while to get at the fence.' He made it finally and set off again with twelve horses in front of him.

When, after jumping the Canal Turn and Valentine's, Buckingham realised he was in front he was so far ahead of the pursuers that he knew he must win if Foinavon kept his feet, and Foinavon's jumping had been safe if slow to that point. Packed Home, Aussie and Greek Scholar had needed only two tries at the twenty-third and it was Biddlecombe's mount who appeared to be the only possible danger as Foinavon jumped the third from home, before crossing the Melling Road. He began to tire, however, and Honey End moved past him on the run towards the last. Brian had found that Red Alligator, in no way put off by his difficulties, was jumping impeccably and finishing more strongly than anything else in the race.

At the last he had reached Packed Home, Solbina, Aussie and Scottish Final but was still behind Greek Scholar. Honey End was a dozen lengths or so ahead of him at the elbow, with just over a furlong to run, yet he reduced that deficit to three lengths by the time they reached the line. Foinavon was an official eighteen lengths in front of him.

Afterwards, Josh Gifford was convinced that Honey End would have won outright had Popham Down not decided to call it a day at the twenty-third. The film of the race does not back him up, for Red Alligator was catching him all the way up the run-in. He, in fact, was the unluckiest horse of all and a disconsolate Brian Fletcher felt that he might never again have such a wonderful chance of winning the National.

Still, Brian had shown himself to be a young rider of extraordinary ability, able to ride a strong finish at the end of four and a half miles. And Red Alligator had run so well that Denys Smith was sure to aim him at the 1968 Grand National. Meanwhile, he would be given two more outings before having a well-earned rest. In the first, at Wetherby, with Brian able to claim his 3 lb. allowance, Red Alligator was beaten four lengths by Castle Falls, who had finished fourteenth in the National. In the other, at Wetherby on Whit Monday, Red Alligator was in the lead when falling three fences from home.

These two performances left a deep impression on the young Fletcher. 'Once a horse has been to Liverpool, he has this thing at the back of his mind : is he going out to jump those big obstacles again? He knows what he has attempted to do, if he has not actually succeeded, and he is never again the same horse.'

Red Alligator did not shake this conviction despite the events of March 30 the next year. Red Rum five years later did not do so either for Red Rum, says Brian, is a law unto himself.

CHAPTER THREE

Red Rum ended his first season of racing on September 25, 1967, with a moderate fourth place in a one-mile Leicester nursery. Five days later Red Alligator and Brian Fletcher, by now without an allowance, began a new campaign at Hexham in Northumberland.

Freddie, second in the 1965 and 1966 Grand Nationals, was set to concede 25 lb. to him and was nearing the end of the road. So when Red Alligator made up ground steadily in the last mile, led at the last and won by two lengths his rider was not greatly impressed. He knew that the race had taken little winning. It was a surprise to many people when, at 3 to 1 favourite, Red Alligator was beaten just over 20 lengths in a three-mile chase at Ayr. But it wasn't a surprise to his rider and, though he was made favourite again at Doncaster in November, he again finished more than 20 lengths behind the winner.

Denys Smith then gave Red Alligator a rest with a view to bringing him back to a short campaign leading to the Grand National. Donald McCain was to take a similar line with Red Rum five years later.

Before Red Alligator reappeared after his mid-winter rest, at Haydock for the Greenall Whitley National Trial, Brian felt that his chance of winning the National on him was far less rosy than it had been the year before. 'He had not shown the same sparkle. He was a stone better horse the year before. In the back of his mind was the thought that he was going to have to jump the Liverpool fences every time he went out and to some extent his confidence had gone.'

Haydock is a good trial course for Liverpool because of the drop on the landing side of some of the fences and a lively performance in the Greenall Whitley would have raised Brian's hopes. They stayed as they were, for Red Alligator jumped deliberately and at no time was going well enough to look like justifying the support of those brave people whose money had made him favourite yet again. There were three weeks to go to the National and Denys Smith decided to send him to Liverpool without another race.

On the Tuesday before the big day, Brian had a disappointing ride on one of the two joint favourites in a selling hurdle at Doncaster and was back at the South Yorkshire course the next day for rides in the only two National Hunt races on the mixed card.

The programme began with a selling handicap on the flat for three-year-olds and among the 20 runners was Red Rum. He had received mild praise in the Timeform weekly issues towards the end of the previous season : 'Has trained on well; stays a mile; acts on firm going.' The Timeform rating of 82 was a high one for a selling plater and it was no surprise to Tim Molony when Red Rum was allotted top weight in the Waterdale Selling Handicap. Several of the runners, however, appeared to have the better of him at the weights, according to Timeform.

This fact, if noted, did not deter his connections from supporting him and after opening at 9 to 2, with 8 to 1 offered bar him, Red Rum's price closed to 11 to 4. Geoff Lewis had the ride and Red Rum was drawn among the favoured high numbers. The ground was reasonably fast and Molony had given Red Rum plenty of work.

Red Rum was one of the fastest away from the stalls and went into the lead two furlongs out as the rank outsider, Mexican Mirth, began to weaken. Duo, the only one seriously backed to beat him, ranged alongside him below the distance but could not get his head in front. Red Rum, hard ridden, battled on to win by a head.

The distance of seven furlongs was, possibly, just short of what Red Rum really required but the same could be said of

17

Duo who later made all the running to win over a mile. Among those watching Red Rum's return to the unsaddling enclosure was Brian Fletcher. Brian had also seen him win at Liverpool the previous March and had made a mental note of the gelding.

'Maybe it was because Red Rum, the name, reminded me of Red Alligator. Anyway, even then he was a good-looking stamp of a horse. Later, of course, he developed into one of the best-looking horses in training but even as a three-year-old there was a lot to like about him.'

Perhaps because of his good looks as well as his stout-hearted victory, there was plenty of competition for Red Rum at the auction following the Doncaster race. Eventually, Tim Molony made the successful bid at 1,400 guineas and Red Rum returned to his stables near Melton Mowbray his job well done. Mr Maurice Kingsley had wanted the trainer to buy him a horse capable of winning a seller and Red Rum had exceeded the specification by winning two and a nursery. The handicapper now had a firm hold on Red Rum and the time had come to sell.

Before any firm arrangements were made, he would run Red Rum at Liverpool on Grand National day where he would have to carry a 10 lb. penalty in a non-seller, the Earl of Sefton's Handicap.

While Red Rum was beginning his journey from Doncaster to Melton Mowbray, young Brian Fletcher was recording a double. Young Ash Leaf, a horse who was to have a profound effect on Brian's riding career and indirectly to bring about his association with Red Rum, easily won the Grey Friars Hurdle and Autobiography, whom Brian rode for Joe Lisle, a very successful owner with Denys Smith, galloped to a 12-length win in the Clock Corner Chase. Young Ash Leaf was trained at that time by Ernie Weymes at Leyburn, one of an increasing number of trainers booking Brian.

He moved on from Doncaster to Liverpool, for the opening day of the Grand National meeting where he had outside rides in the two races open to professional National Hunt jockeys. In the Lancashire Hurdle, Golden Duck attracted little money in the betting despite a win in an Ayr Handicap on his previous run, but Brian sent him to the front two flights out and he won by eight lengths. He was in a confident and happy frame of mind as he went out to ride J.F.K. on the Friday. The seven-year-old had won nicely the time before and was favourite to win the Mildmay Chase.

The Mildmay course, constructed as a Grand National course in miniature, has claimed too many victims for it to be regarded as other than a testing trial. J.F.K. misjudged the first fence of all and crashed heavily, giving Brian a bad fall. Concussed, he seemed for a time to have little chance of partnering Red Alligator the next day. Resilience, however, is a feature of his physical and mental make-up and on the Saturday morning he was to be found in the Turkish Baths at Southport along with several of the other jockeys who had mounts in the National. They were there to try to shed a few pounds and avoid adding to the burden imposed by the handicapper. Brian could do bottom weight, which Red Alligator was set to carry, with ease. He was there to trim off a pound or two so that he would not put up overweight on a Denys Smith five-year-old, Look North, in the Maghull Stakes run on the flat later in the day.

His presence in the Baths caused a little concern to some of the more experienced jockeys, John Lawrence included. 'He politely accepted our fatherly advice on the dangers of spending too long in the steam room, lost the necessary pounds to "do" 9 st. 7 lb., and went out to ride a race no Aintree veteran could have bettered,' wrote Lawrence later in his account of the National.

Seventy minutes before Red Rum made what was to be his final appearance in a flat race, Brian paraded in front of the packed stands on Red Alligator. Despite his indifferent record since the National of the year before, Red Alligator started joint third favourite. The clear first choice was Different Class, a horse who had started his career in Yorkshire point-to-point races. He had been considered one of the unlucky ones in the Foinavon fiasco, having been well placed and going strongly when put out of the race at the twenty-third. He had shown no ill-effects from his Aintree exertions and had won three of his four races before going to Liverpool. David Mould had the ride and was optimistic about his chances.

Rutherfords, winner over the stiff Wetherby three and a half miles and trained by Neville Crump at Middleham, was second favourite and there was plenty of public money for Bassnet, the beaten favourite of the year before, The Fossa and Moidore's Token.

Red Alligator did not give any obvious sign during the long parade that he was remembering his experience of the previous year and as the 45 runners fanned out across the course and were brought under orders Brian again prepared to follow Terry Biddlecombe's advice.

The going was perfect, the sun was shining and the crowd had every reason to expect a fast-run race. Foinavon, carrying 5 lb. overweight, had a new rider and carried numerous small bets from those who believed lightning could strike twice in the same place, but the more knowledgeable reasoned that if he could not go the pace as a nine-year-old he was unlikely to do so at ten and the bookmakers shared that view. They made him a 66 to 1 shot.

The pace was a sensible one on the long run to the first, where Ford Ord overjumped and fell. Beecham went at the third, leaving 43 horses to go to Becher's at a gallop later described by the jockeys as nice and steady. Valbus, The Fossa, Princeful and Rutherfords were disputing the lead. Red Alligator was towards the outside and in the centre of the cavalry charge. He was jumping safely, too safely for his jockey's liking. 'He knew what he had to do and was making sure that he took care of himself. He wasn't having a go, as he had done the year before, and at Liverpool it pays for a horse to have a go,' says Brian.

'If horses are slovenly in the air at Liverpool they lose too much time and can get into a lot of trouble. Undoubtedly, Red Alligator was remembering the size of the obstacles from the 1973 race.'

Becher's Brook for once lived up to this reputation as the most testing of the fences. Six horses went down there, including What a Myth. Last of the six to go was Polaris Missile and he crumped to the ground in the path of Red Alligator. Remarkably, Red Alligator was able to pick up again immediately after landing and clear his fallen rival. He was now nearer last than first and Brian decided to move him nearer to the leaders. By the time they reached the Chair, Red Alligator was in twelfth place, and within reach of The Fossa, Rondetto, Rutherfords,

Moidore's Token and Different Class, who were in the van of the 31 still standing.

Foinavon, astonishingly to most of the spectators at home and on the racecourse, was close behind him and going well. But Liverpool had handed out all the luck to him the year before and this time gave him a helping of misfortune. At the water, that most innocuous of fences, Bassnet was knocked sideways and into the water and Foinavon, Ronald's Boy and Champion Prince were put out of the race.

Red Alligator's ultra-safe jumping did not prevent him from continuing his progress towards the leaders and at the second Becher's he had The Fossa, Rondetto, Different Class, Rutherfords, Princeful and Moidore's Token in his sights. Rondetto went at the twenty-third for the second year running and Red Alligator took the Canal Turn in Sixth place. Valentine's Brook is the next fence, the sixth from home, and by the time they reached that Brian was beginning to have thoughts of victory.

David Mould led on Different Class at Valentine's and in Brian's eyes Different Class was going extremely well. He pushed up Red Alligator to join him at the next plain fence and hit the front at the plain fence which followed. Mould was still full of confidence on Different Class but as Red Alligator galloped on relentlessly and took a definite lead at the third from home Different Class suddenly came off the bit.

'He found virtually nothing,' Brian recalls,' and I knew that bar a fall I would win. I was certain that my horse would sprint away from the last because he had only 10 st. on his back and I hadn't asked him to do anything up to then.'

Red Alligator met both the twenty-ninth and last fences perfectly and tackled the run-in with relish, increasing his margin over the brave Different Class with every stride. Ridden out with hands and heels, he led by 20 lengths at the post where Moidore's Token snatched second place from Different Class. The time was a fast one, confirming that in following Terry Biddlecombe's strategy Brian had given Red Alligator exemplary assistance. Far better for a Grand National winner to finish full of running than near to exhaustion.

So in only his third season as a professional, Brian had achieved an ambition which had been with him in early childhood. It was a great achievement, too, for Denys Smith and a moment to savour for Mr John Manners, a butcher and near neighbour of the trainer at Bishop Auckland. Like Anglo, Red Alligator was bred by a Downpatrick farmer, William Kennedy, from a 70 guineas mare, Miss Alligator. She had brought her low price at Dublin only three years after finishing sixth to Musidora in the Oaks. Mr Kennedy got £140 for Anglo as a foal and 360 guineas for Red Alligator as a yearling. Anglo's owner and Mr Manners each received towards £18,000 for their victories at Aintree alone.

Brian answered the many questions fired at him at the post-National Press conference with all the modesty which was to characterise his career, and then made his way to the weighing room next door to change out of the colours which he was to wear in two more Grand Nationals and into those for Look North. He was in time to see Lester Piggott weigh out before the Earl of Sefton Stakes in which he was to ride Red Rum.

Low numbers have the advantage over the Liverpool mile and Red Rum was drawn highest of the 20 runners. Yet despite this and his 10 lb. penalty, he was made a clear favourite. Only one of the others had been out previously and this was Adam's Pet, trained by Ron Barnes at Warrington and ridden by a very promising apprentice, Clive Eccleston. Piggott was well away on Red Rum and turning into the straight, with half a mile to go, had him in third place. Queen's Route, one of the two leaders, was beaten shortly afterwards but the other, Ladrap, hung on until below the distance. Here Piggott delivered his challenge but Alan's Pet, making his run at the same time, gained a fractional lead and retained it to the line.

Eccleston's 5 lb. allowance and Red Rum's penalty had taken him 18 lb. above Allan's Pet in the weights. Yet as two-year-olds there had been only 5 lb. between them in the Timeform ratings, Alan's Pet having won a maiden race at Doncaster. It was, therefore, a wonderfully good run by Red Rum to get within a short head of the filly in the light of his previous performances. Clearly, he was training on and there could be more races to be won with him, perhaps over longer distances than a mile.

It was not to be. Mr Kingsley wanted to sell and got in touch with Robert Renton, who had trained Freebooter to win the 1950 Grand National and all the other major chases run over the Aintree course. Robert Renton had his stables at

Oxclose, just outside Ripon in Yorkshire, and he had turned out a steady stream of National Hunt winners in post-war years. Mrs Lurline Brotherton had owned Freebooter and he was on the look-out for a potential chaser for her.

While Mr Kingsley was confirming in his mind the decision to sell Red Rum in the minutes following his narrow defeat by Alan's Pet, Brian Fletcher was weighing out to ride Look North. At 2,000 guineas, a five times more expensive horse than Red Rum, Look North had been well beaten in his one race the previous season.

This unimposing record did not represent the gelding's true ability, the bookmakers ruled, and he opened at only 4 to 1. At the off, he was second favourite but he did not at any stage of the race suggest that he would repay his rider's visit to the Turkish Baths. Still, the celebrations at the customary Grand National dinner were to come. Red Alligator would be the toast. Red Rum had five years of racing and a lot to learn before his name, too, would be on everyone's lips at the cele-bration dinner.

CHAPTER FOUR

When Robert Renton drove down from Yorkshire to Tim Molony's yard, he was prepared to have a wasted day. But when Red Rum was led out for him to see he took an immediate liking to him. 'He was a real compact, good-looking horse then as he is now, and so I bought him.' The price was £1,200, as opposed to the 1,400 guineas to which his owner had had to go to buy him in at Liverpool. Robert Renton was convinced that Red Rum had the physique to make a chaser and that Mrs Lurline Brotherton had a bargain.

That conviction grew even firmer when he got Red Rum back to Oxclose. 'He always used to kick out for quite a long time when someone got on him at home yet it was just high spirits. He was a very temperate animal and never once caused trouble in or out of his stable in the time that I had him,' his first National Hunt trainer states.

He handed over Red Rum to a girl to 'do'. Sandra Kendall had been with Robert Renton for six years, ever since leaving school in her nearby home town of Ripon. Sandra's early experience had been gained with her own ponies and in her early 'teens she used to ride one of them, Tammy, to Oxclose where her brother worked as a stableboy. She rode well enough for the trainer to allow her to ride out with his string and, by the time she was fifteen, and due to leave school, she was riding out regularly.

Good stable labour has never been easy to acquire and Robert Renton persuaded her to join his force full time, straight from school. She loved the life and cared deeply for the horses put in her charge. Even now that women riders have been granted the opportunity to ride in flat races, and to compete against men, there remains an overwhelming school of thought that they will never become serious rivals to the professionals of the opposite sex. Surprisingly, some of the leading women share that opinion though as women have proved capable of beating the top men, consistently, in the more exacting worlds of show-jumping and three-day eventing, it is difficult to see why they should not become at least as proficient as jockeys.

Just as there are men who stand out in the crowd of jockeys populating our racecourses, so are there women of above-average ability. As they are given more opportunities to race-ride, so will they develop their art and it could be that trainers in the future will turn to the ladies when they have a horse who is not responding to the masculine touch. There have been examples already : Desperate Dee, for instance, appeared to have lost his enthusiasm for racing if not his ability until Joan Calvert rode him in a mixed race at York. Desperate Dee jumped out of his stall with what had become uncharacteristic alacrity, and proceeded to run his rivals into the ground.

Back in the sixties there were trainers who ruled out stable-girls because they thought they lacked the strength to impose their will on a lively thoroughbred, as though strength rather than understanding and sympathy was the prime requisite. Presumably, their arrogance extended to their believing also that courage was a male quality alone. Robert Renton was not one of them.

Sandra had been in charge of several useful horses before Red Rum appeared at Oxclose, notably Dagmar Gittell, a successful chaser. And although Red Rum let it be known straight away that the antics which, in retrospect, had been summed up by Tim Molony as 'gay' made him a difficult ride, Robert Renton had no hesitation in nominating her to take him over.

'It was marvellous to get him,' says Sandra. 'He was like a little lamb in his box – a perfect gentleman, in fact – except that he played about over the box door. He used to be playful occasionally when he was being groomed, but he never kicked to hurt.'

Once out of his box, his liveliness manifested itself more noticeably. 'He was always on the go and there wasn't a day passed by that he wasn't bucking and kicking.' The gallops used by the Renton string were down by the side of a river and were reached from Oxclose via a tarmac road. It provided only an insecure footing for a wayward thoroughbred, and wayward Red Rum certainly was.

'We always had a job to get down there with him; it was so slippery. He nearly came down a few times. But I got used to his bucks and he never had me off once. Mind you, nobody else liked to ride him.'

Even when behaving at his worst, Red Rum had his ears forward, not back, and to Sandra there was no evil intent at all. 'He used to buck and squeal for the enjoyment of it. He was never sour.' The bucking continued when Red Rum was cantered. 'It stopped only when we were doing fast work. He couldn't manage it then.'

After the work had finished and the string returned to Oxclose some of the horses were dismounted and led back up the lane. But not Red Rum. On the very few occasions that Sandra tried this, he reared and jumped and did his best to break away from her. The solution was to ride him right up to his box.

Later in his career, Red Rum showed an uncompromising reluctance to skip over hurdles at home but to the three-year-old Red Rum they offered a welcome variation from routine and he demonstrated an above-average prowess at getting from one side of a hurdle to the other. His introduction to his first small obstacle came the day after his arrival at Oxclose.

Sandra remembers it well: 'I was told to take him to the back paddock, where we had this little learner's fence, and pop him over it. In view of what he was behaving like on the roads, I thought I was in for the fright of my life, but he never batted an eyelid. I cantered him up to it, without a lead, and he just flew over it. Then we took him over the big ones, with a couple more to keep him company and he never hesitated. He was the perfect hurdler.'

When, as Sandra adds, Red Rum got older and wiser, Robert Renton did not attempt to school him before the start of a season. Occasionally, she would take him down to the schooling paddock where the other hurdlers were busy. 'There was some nettles and he would say, "Blow you." So I left it at that.'

Cheltenham was a course often visited by Robert Renton and its first meeting of 1968 was chosen by him for the introduction of two juvenile hurdlers. Tommy Stack, a young Irishman who had joined the Ripon trainer as an amateur two seasons previsiously, was to ride Naughty Story in the first division of the Junior Novices' Hurdle and Josh Gifford, regarded as one of the top handful of hurdle jockeys in Britain, was to partner Red Rum in the second division.

Sandra's brother used to drive the horsebox and she always travelled with Red Rum to his races. The journey to Gloucestershire necessitated a stay overnight in the racecourse stables. Red Rum was not a very good traveller and he became anxious when in a strange box, a combination of demerits which must have been against his chance in the races at far-away courses. 'I found that he was all right in the horsebox provided he could see you and that you made a lot of fuss of him, but he was always on the go and sweated up badly when put in a box other than his own. He was a nervous horse.' Any apprehension she felt about his physical well-being that first night at Cheltenham, however, largely disappeared when he ate as heartily as ever.

That was to be an outstanding characteristic of Red Rum throughout his early career and to the present day. 'I don't think he ever left an oat in all the time that I had him,' Sandra states.

The riding arrangements that particular day reflected what was thought of the chances of the two Renton-trained horses: Naughty Story had been well beaten in his two races on the flat that year and would be a rank outsider; Red Rum's flat form, allied to his looks, would ensure him a leading place in the betting against opposition which did not appear strong.

The going was good on September 18 at Cheltenham, where the programme began with a selling chase. There was a close finish, followed by an objection in that race but the stewards decided that the result should stand, and so Brian Fletcher recorded his first victory over the famous course. He also rode the well-fancied Geordie Lad against Naughty Story and came within three-quarters of a length of completing a double.

Naughty Story led for a long way, and then faded towards the rear of the field.

Favourite for the second division was Acastus, trained by Fulke Walwyn and a winner already at Ludlow. His price hardened to 13 to 8 as Red Rum's drifted from 5 to 1 to 8 to 1, though none looked better than him in the parade ring. The blinkered Double Diamond led at the first and then was over-taken by Red Rum. Rob Lad, a complete outsider, took up the running from Red Rum at halfway but whereas Rob Lad quickly retreated when headed by Acastus after taking the third last, Red Rum hung on.

At the last, he still had a chance but the slight increase of pace mustered by Acastus was enough to shake him off. He finished second, five lengths behind and six lengths in front of the third horse, another with previous hurdling experience. Red Rum had earned £90 and given his owner and trainer considerable hope for the future.

'He ran a heck of a race,' the devoted Sandra recalls, though her pleasure in Red Rum's achievement was more than offset by one aspect of it. Having been given the Lester Piggott treatment on the flat, Red Rum knew what happened at the business end of a race yet as Roberto, after his Derby victory, and Vincent O'Brien, his Irish trainer, could testify the bark of the Piggott whip is worse then its bite. Sandra, on the evidence of that Cheltenham race, thinks otherwise about the whip as wielded by Josh Gifford. It had a marked effect on Red Rum, so marked that she thought Red Rum might be permanently soured against racing.

Inevitably, there is something of a conflict between a jockey out to win a race and the 'lad' – girl or boy, woman or man – whose task in life is to keep the horse in question at the peak of fitness and in a happy frame of mind. The lad becomes so involved with the horse that any suggestion of severe usage is anathema, and yet a jockey can use the whip as a harsh – and to some – necessary form of encouragement.

Josh Gifford had been told that Red Rum was a lazy horse who needed reminders from the whip to persuade him to try his hardest. Just as the parent may be too close to the child to see his faults and to apply discipline, the lad can be too close to the horse and yet the opinions of the parent and of the stablelad must be taken on their merits. Sandra's reaction to Josh Gifford, as to most of the many jockeys who rode Red Rum in those early days of his National Hunt career was, she admits, slightly hostile. She believed he was being given a hard time in his races. And she thought, and still thinks, that a more subtle approach, taking into account Red Rum's likes and dislikes, could have had a more beneficial effect.

'He was a funny sort of horse and he didn't like to be boxed in at all in a race. He didn't like to be even touched – at the back, gently, or near the front, that was where he liked to be.' She had the temerity to voice her opinion at Oxclose and it did tie in to some extent with that of Paddy Broderick, who was to take over the riding of Red Rum later in the season. Josh Gifford, in fact, was not asked to ride Red Rum again.

After Cheltenham, Red Rum was due to run at Ascot but was withdrawn when the ground was made very heavy by continuous rain. He then went to the Lincolnshire course, Market Rasen, for another three-year-old hurdle.

The ground was on the soft side of good and as such suited one of the smallest horses in the race, Francophile, a winner at York as a two-year-old and a stone or more superior to Red Rum on the flat on his best form. Francophile was trained at Malton by Frank Carr, a likeable and modest man who for a time had been so disenchanted with racing that he gave up his job as a stable lad and went into a York chocolate factory.

Frank invariably trains a few hurdlers to help keep his staff happy during the winter and, more often than not, those hurdlers win more than their share of races. Francophile, despite making errors at two or three of the hurdles that day at Market Rasen, sustained a good gallop in the lead from half way and won comfortably. Red Rum made a bad mistake at the third last, lost ground, and was beaten by two lengths for third place.

Andy Turnell was Red Rum's jockey at Market Rasen and Robert Renton went to the top again when he next ran Red Rum, at Nottingham in November. This time Johnny Cook was engaged. Francophile was in the field again for what was one of the most valuable three-year-old hurdles of the season, the Merit Hurdle. So, too, was Red Rum's Cheltenham conqueror, Acastus, and seven horses who had won their last races. These included Red Rum's old adversary on the flat, Soloning, now with Fred Winter and developing into an altogether more promising National Hunt prospect than he had been with no obstacles to negotiate.

Soloning it was who won the race, albeit narrowly from Francophile. Red Rum, in the middle division until beyond halfway, made up ground on the leaders in the last half mile and more than lived up to expectations by gaining third place, three lengths behind Francophile and four lengths in front of Acastus. Third-place money was £109.

Red Rum had yet another new jockey, T. S. Murphy, when he had his fourth hurdles outing at Doncaster later the same month. As was to be expected after the Nottingham performance, he started favourite for the second division of a three-year-old hurdle which had been chosen by Fred Rimell for the début of a good-looking bay called Coral Diver.

Red Rum disputed the lead with Coral Diver and Rare Comedy, from the Peter Easterby stable, at the second last but could not quicken on the soft ground and was beaten into third place. A disappointing result on the face of it though not in the light of what the first two were to achieve subsequently. Coral Diver won the £5,000 Victor Ludorum Hurdle at Haydock and the *Daily Express* Triumph Hurdle at Cheltenham, the supreme championship for first-season hurdlers. Rare Comedy made less startling progress but still was good enough to win a handicap at Newcastle when the only four-year-old among 18 runners.

Robert Renton was well pleased with Red Rum's initial campaign and did not race him again until early March, when once more he opposed Rare Comedy and Francophile. John Doyle, son of the Wetherby trainer and former jockey, Tony Doyle, were retained by Mrs Brotherton for a while and Tony was given the ride in the Harewood Hurdle, for four-year-olds. Red Rum was easy to back at 10 to 1 after his four-match lay-off and ran accordingly, being left behind by the leading group in the straight. At the post he was a dozen or so lengths behind the winner – Rare Comedy.

After that, Robert Renton decided to fly high again and send Red Rum to Liverpool for the Lancashire Hurdle, not one of the best-endowed events for four-year-olds but one of the most difficult to win. It was to be his sixth race for the Ripon trainer and he was to have his sixth jockey, an Irishman, Paddy

30

Broderick. Paddy had been in demand by most of the North-country trainers and had ridden winners for such as Frank Carr and Denys Smith. His style was similar to that of Stan Mellor – not out of the textbook for flat-race apprentices but very effective when it came to getting the maximum response from a tired horse. He was, and still is, a fine horseman.

Colin Davies, the Chepstow trainer, saddled Clever Scot for the race and although he started at 100 to 8 there was good reason for confidence behind him. He had been in the lead when falling at the second-last flight in the Triumph Hurdle at Cheltenham. Brian Fletcher was riding him and his orders were to see that the pace was a good one. Following out those orders, he went into the lead at the second flight, with Red Rum among those keeping him company.

The pace was indeed a good one and, when Brian asked for and got an extra surge of effort from Clever Scot between the last two flights, there was nothing that Paddy Broderick could do about it. Clever Scot won by ten lengths. Yet Red Rum beat Lord Tom for third place and Lord Tom had a run a good third with 11 st. 10 lb. in a handicap at Newbury before that.

'They were over the moon about him, considering how he had run before that, but they thought I made a bit too much use of him,' Paddy Broderick remembers. 'Yet I think that was always the way to ride him; to let him run his own race. He wasn't too genuine at that time, I thought.'

Mild criticism or not, Paddy was engaged again when Red Rum made his next appearance, eleven days later at Wetherby. Apart from New Brighton, first at Nottingham in his previous outing, the 21 opponents of Red Rum were unimposing in the extreme and the surprise is that Red Rum was not at shorter odds than 15 to 8. He was entitled to be at odds on. Brian Fletcher was on New Brighton and on this occasion was able to listen to applause for Red Rum without any sense of exulta-tion, for Red Rum mastered his mount decisively in the final quarter of a mile.

'I had let him run his own race again,' says Paddy. And his assessment of Red Rum's requirements had been proved right.

The time had come now to move into handicaps and the Wetherby victory brought Red Rum a 7 lb. penalty for his next objective, the Bradmore Handicap Hurdle at Nottingham. The ground was good, as it had been at Wetherby, and it was being recognised that such going suited him well, though there was no suggestion that he had any distinct preference.

'I was always up there, in front, until I made a bad mistake at the last. I would be a length and a half behind At Ease after that and got back and won half a length. And At Ease was a good handicap hurdler at the time,' Paddy recalls.

Another ten-day gap and then Robert Renton took Red Rum to Teesside Park, a course whose amenities do not match the excellence of its track. The racecourse executive, however, have had great difficulties to face over proposed road development and deserve enormous credit for keeping Teeside on the racing map.

Red Rum carried a 5 lb. penalty that day late in an April which had seen plenty of rain. The official description of the going was 'Soft: patchy'. Paddy remembers it as being very soft indeed. Red Rum's two later trainers were to be unwavering in their belief that he could not gallop effectively on soft ground but the man on top at Teesside would not have agreed with them. 'He went along on that, at that time, as easy as he did on any other kind of ground.'

The race remains clear in his memory: 'I held him up a bit that day and hit the front coming to the straight because I had to go for the outside to get the better ground. I beat Kit Stobbs, on Rigton Prince, to it and he had to stay on my inside. He was looking for the best ground as well.

'Red Rum thought then that he had done all he had to do. That was it. And I had to work very hard on him to keep him going.' Rigton Prince, just preferred to Red Rum in the market after an easy win at Hexham, battled it out with him all the way down the straight but Paddy's perseverance carried the day. Red Rum won by a neck.

The Ayr May meeting was chosen for Red Rum's final appearance of his first National Hunt season. Golden Berry, in the same colours as Red Rum, won a novice hurdle on the first day in the hands of Tommy Stack but Paddy Broderick was entrusted with the ride on Red Rum again in the Orchardton Handicap Hurdle on the second day. Nothing Higher, fifth in the Scottish Champion Hurdle over the course and distance the month before, was joint favourite with Geordie Lad, the mount of Brian Fletcher. Red Rum opened out in the betting as favourite but eased two points and started as joint third favourite.

The fact that Paddy had held up Red Rum at Teesside and that the tactics had met with success had added weight to Robert Renton's belief that he should be ridden in that way in all his races. Accordingly, he instructed Paddy to hold him up again. 'I did as I was told. I held him up, and kept him on the inside, and the horse didn't like it; he got sickened. He just wouldn't do it for me. He used to love bowling along in the first two or three. Whatever he wanted to do, let him do it – that was my opinion on how he should be ridden,' Paddy adds.

While Paddy was restraining Red Rum on the inside, his fellow Irishman, Ron Barry, was setting a good gallop on Patrona. Geordie Lad moved into a challenging position before the last, where Patrona began to weaken, but was outpaced on the run-in by a 20 to 1 chance, Paidfor, ridden by Ken White. Red Rum, not having been allowed to gallop on when he wanted to, steadfastly refused to increase his speed when the request came and trailed in towards the tail of the field.

'We were all saying that he wasn't honest,' says Paddy, some-what reluctantly, as he looks back to those races on Red Rum. 'But when you think about it he was a stayer racing in two-mile handicap hurdles and they were not far enough for him. He must have been a good horse then to win such races. Be-cause he was a stayer, you had to make use of him and go your own gallop because he just stayed and stayed. When I rode him as I wanted to and had him in the first two or three, he would be going easy but when you asked him to go he couldn't go any faster.'

After the Ayr failure, Red Rum was retired for the season. Paddy Broderick rode him only once more, at Doncaster the following November. He already had three feeble performances behind him and though set to receive 8 lb. from At Ease was a weak 100 to 8 shot, whereas At Ease was second favourite. 'He ran a mother's race on me that day,' Paddy states. 'At Ease passed me at the second last, running away. To me the horse was a bit sick and wasn't doing everything he could do.'

Paddy retained a great admiration, nevertheless, for Red Rum's character. 'He was tough and he used to play about and enjoy himself. You could let him do that.' And he knew the horse had plenty of ability and one day would make a chaser – 'But I never ever thought that he would win a National. Yet he became a tremendous horse.' Paddy was not the only one intimately concerned with Red Rum to be astonished by his later exploits.

CHAPTER FIVE

When his first season of hurdling was completed, Red Rum was roughed off and then turned out in a field at the back of the stables at Oxclose. 'I don't think he knew what grass was,' says Sandra Kendall. 'He didn't do at all well that first summer.' She took him a bucket-full of corn every night and he devoured it as quickly as he had when stabled.

His break was not long one and by mid-September he was racing again. Cheltenham's September meeting the previous season had been the occasion for the first of ten outings; the corresponding fixture in 1969 was chosen for his first outing again and this time it was to be the first of fourteen. Tommy Stack by now was established as stable jockey and he was to have the ride.

One of the charming incongruities about National Hunt racing, a highly dangerous pastime, is that the jockeys preserve an overt cheerfulness which is as genuine as Wedgwood Benn's commitment to nationalisation. They are in many ways an astonishing breed. One of the most cheerful and the most capable is Tommy Stack.

He went to boarding school in his native Ireland and thence to an insurance office in Dublin. His mother hoped he would enter the priesthood and it was not before a deal of discussion and heart-searching, and not without considerable misgivings, that the young Tommy Stack decided against the Church and in favour of racing. He rode as an amateur in Ireland and that experience fired him with a determination to try to get to the

35

top as a jump jockey. He wrote to Robert Renton, asking for the opportunity to ride out for him, and the Ripon trainer – the son of a clergyman – was glad to accede to the request. He sent his butler to meet Tommy at the Leeds-Bradford Airport, after his flight from Dublin, and so began what was to be a profitable association for both trainer and jockey.

Tommy rode five winners in his first season with the stable and eleven in his second, and turned professional before his third, the 1967–68 season. During Red Rum's novice hurdle days, Tommy heard plenty of talk about the horse – 'they thought a great deal about him' – and also heard the conversation become far from complimentary on occasions. He did not get to know Red Rum then, however, for Sandra alone was his partner at home and he was not one of the seven jockeys chosen to ride him in races.

Having shown himself to be perfectly adept at jumping hurdles, Red Rum was not asked to school at Oxclose before being sent to Cheltenham and, in fact, had not done a great deal of work. He was one of only two four-year-olds in the Andoversford Handicap Hurdle, which attracted twenty-one runners. He was virtually ignored in the betting and in the race was at no stage near enough to the leaders to give any hope that he would finish in the frame.

Neither trainer nor jockey felt any despondency over the display because Red Rum clearly was not fully fit. He would do better next time out, it was thought, at Doncaster. John Doyle, his allowance down to 5 lb., took over from Tommy in the Town Field Handicap Hurdle on October 25 and once again Red Rum was one of two four-year-olds opposing older horses. Dunela, who had won the Cheltenham race, was 6 lb. worse off with Red Rum this time and there were only six points between them in the betting. But whereas Dunela moved through the field in the straight, Red Rum went the other way to finish well out at the back.

That was slightly disturbing for Red Rum's connections and what was to follow at Wetherby was even more so. John Doyle rode him again, a fortnight after Doncaster, in the Tadcaster Handicap Hurdle. The journey to the course was a short one, and although the ground was on the soft side of good it was not deep enough to worry any horse. Four of the twelve runners were preferred to him in the betting, but there was a little money for him and he was thought to be fit enough to do himself full justice.

He didn't. Tommy Stack, riding for the Cheshire trainer, Colin Crossley, landed a fair-sized gamble on Jamoe. Red Rum was in touch with Jamoe until just after halfway and then dropped steadily behind. Paddy Broderick was called upon then to see if his brand of horsemanship and strength in the saddle could bring about a badly needed revival. The race chosen was one confined to four-year-olds and carrying more than £1,000 in prize money at the Doncaster November meeting.

Surprisingly, the handicapper had set Red Rum to concede 3 lb. to Rare Comedy who had beaten him at level weights in the race won by Coral Diver over the same course and distance the previous season, yet the Red Rum of six months ago would have gone very close to winning. The way in which At Ease sauntered past him at the third last was both bewildering and disappointing to Paddy, and the murmurs of discontent about Red Rum's character grew in volume and frequency back at Oxclose.

'Mrs Brotherton began to talk about getting rid of him,' Sandra Kendall recalls. Her attachment to Red Rum was such that any suggestion of selling him came as an outrage, particularly so when she felt that Red Rum's failures were not his fault. 'He had the cough badly at the beginning of the season and he never recovered from it. He could not get going again.

'I kept saying that he was not himself: his bucks weren't as strong. He did buck and jump about but he wasn't half the horse of the season before. But Mr Renton thought I was wrong and the opinion was that Red Rum was going off racing. I was frightened in case they sold him, but that was not why I told them the horse was not right. Red Rum was not to blame for the way he was racing.'

The opinion that Red Rum was not putting his best foot forward was expressed more tangibly when he next ran, in the Dick Whittington Handicap Hurdle at Catterick on New Year's Eve. Blinkers were fitted.

Blinkers are regarded as an aid to lazy and/or ungenerous horses or those whose concentration is inclined to wander. Frequently they have a pronounced beneficial effect the first time they are fitted, and this effect tends to diminish with successive fittings. The description, rogue's badge, is not always fair or accurate in that some horses fitted with blinkers are entirely honest, but if a trainer resorts to using them it means that in some way he is dissatisfied with the horse in question.

Tommy Stack, who had his second ride on the blinkered Red Rum that day at Catterick, remembers that Red Rum was thought to be doing 'not quite one hundred per cent'. At Ease was the 5 to 4 favourite and Red Rum, very surprisingly, was second favourite at 6 to 1 after opening at sevens. The betting accurately foretold the story of the race.

Night Patrol, one of the joint third favourites, led from the start until the turn for home on the final circuit. Red Rum was poised to challenge the new leader, Persian Valor, when Night Patrol weakened and took up the running between the last two flights. Sandra was elated and Tommy Stack hopeful when he jumped the last in front, but along came At Ease to pip him by a length. 'Maybe he wasn't doing quite one hundred per cent again,' says Tommy, though he is not inclined to condemn Red Rum for his performance in that race. Nor does he do so for his run next time out, in heavy ground at Wetherby.

Tommy maintained that Red Rum really did need ground that was 'on top', which did not give way on the surface and hold the feet. It was heavy at Wetherby where, without blinkers, Red Rum ran third to Vulmegan – a winner at Huntingdon the time before – and Huperade, later to oppose Red Rum at Liverpool. The distances were twelve lengths and a length, but Red Rum had Rare Comedy in fourth place and some useful horses further behind.

That race was over two and a half miles, the longest distance he had ever attempted. It took place on a January Tuesday. Doncaster is some thirty miles down the A1 from Wetherby and it was hardly surprising that the ground there on the Friday of the same week should be soft. Nevertheless, Red Rum turned out again to take on Palm Beach, a gelding bred by the Queen and having three successive hurdle victories behind him for Fred Rimell. By the time that Terry Biddlecombe made his forward move on Palm Beach, with three-quarters of a mile to travel, Red Rum was a tired horse and he trailed in at the back.

Robert Renton evidently did not share Tommy Stack's opinion that Red Rum needed sound ground for he started Red Rum in a handicap hurdle at Wetherby fifteen days after Doncaster. January had been a soaker and February began in the same vein. The going was extremely deep as Roy Edwards, deputising for Tommy, cantered Red Rum to the start of the Bishopthorpe Handicap Hurdle on a day which had begun with a win for Brian Fletcher on the ill-fated Dondieu.

The pace set by the apprentice rider of Alby Hill was moderate and, with four flights to jump, six of the seven runners were in contention. Red Rum was the first to fall back towards the already beaten pacemaker and as Supermaster, carrying 12 st. 7 lb., passed the post narrowly in front of Supathene, ridden by Brian Fletcher, Red Rum was struggling along almost twenty lengths behind.

Supermaster, two years older than Red Rum at seven years of age, soon went chasing but Red Rum was asked to soldier on in handicap hurdles and, to the dismay but not surprise of Sandra Kendall, things did not improve for him. The blinkers returned for him at Teesside Park in mid-March when he carried top weight in the £340 Long Dog Handicap Hurdle over two miles five furlongs. Barry Brogan, eventually to have a short spell in one of National Hunt's top jockey jobs, was engaged by Robert Renton and he returned to the weighing room mud-spattered and disconsolate after yet another sub-standard display by Red Rum. Fifth of seven to finish, beaten fifteen lengths, in a relatively poor field was all he was able to achieve in the heavy ground that day. That meant that in nine races Red Rum had won a total of £142 and that in his last three only a handful of horses had finished behind him.

'He was being mugged about something terrible,' says Sandra Kendall, who steadfastly held to her view that Red Rum was not being given a chance to throw off the debilitating effects of the early-season cough. And as Red Rum raced on, and raced badly, she devoted her work time and her spare time to him; I used to molly-coddle him for hours, trying to get him back to his old self.'

'I have never known a horse with such a constitution,' states Tommy Stack. And what a constitution. Four days after plodding through the Teesside mud, Red Rum was on his way to the

Cheltenham Festival meeting where he was to challenge twenty-eight of the best long-distance hurdlers in the country in the George Duller Hurdle. One of them, All Found, had run second at Sandown on the Friday – the day of Teesside – but he was a fresh horse having had only three races that season. And he started favourite. Anyone wanting 33 to 1 about Red Rum would have been accommodated by eager bookmakers, though officially he was returned among the '25 to 1 others'. Roy Edwards rode him again and had to put up 4 lb. overweight, Red Rum having been allotted bottom weight.

The stable regarded him by now as lazy and as liable to run his race in snatches and the George Duller did nothing to make them retract their opinions. After being towards the rear of the field to halfway, Red Rum suddenly began to overhaul horse after horse so that he had reached a challenging position as he turned into the straight for the last time, with the daunting hill to come. He still was in touch with All Found, Vulmegan and Albinella as they came to the final flight and then weakened to finish out of the first six. His display contrasted with that of his fellow five-year-old, Soloning, whose career so often crossed paths with that of Red Rum. He won the Arkle Challenge Trophy Chase thirty-five minutes before the George Duller in the style of a future champion.

Almost a month went by before Sandra Kendall prepared Red Rum for yet another journey to Cheltenham, this time for the two-and-a-half-mile Ronald Royds Handicap Hurdle. Tommy Stack resumed his partnership with Red Rum on ground that he was convinced was too soft for him. For a reason not apparent in the formbook, the opening price of Red Rum was 5 to 1 and he started third favourite to Irish Special, who was on a hat-trick, and Say Who You Are, a fair staying handicapper.

Say Who You Are tried to duck round the side of the fifth hurdle and Irish Special strode away to a good victory. Red Rum was never in a position to take advantage of any mistake by a leader and a well-beaten sixth was the best he could manage. For a horse who was not a particularly good traveller Red Rum was spending a lot of time on the road and away from home. And for his next race a mere ten days after Cheltenham, he journeyed up to Perth.

'He was never right after the cough,' Tommy Stack recalls. 'But by that time we were getting quite fed up with him.' Sandra Kendall was growing increasingly perturbed about the talk of selling Red Rum and increasingly anxious about his poor performances, yet she kept telling herself that Red Rum was not to blame. She would have been far happier had the decision been made to retire him for the season and give him a good rest. That, she believed, was what he needed.

In the box on the way to Perth, she saw to it that Red Rum was kept as relaxed as possible and she hoped that the drop in class which running him in the Perthshire Drag Hunt Handicap Hurdle entailed would at least see him restore a vestige of his reputation.

It was late April and the ground had dried out sufficiently to merit the description 'good'. Tommy Stack held him in the middle of the small field until halfway and was hard at work on him more than two flights from home. The distance of three miles was the longest Red Rum had ever attempted and it contributed to his greatly-improved display. At two and a half miles he would have been comfortably held by Tabix, but he ran on to such purpose towards the end that he caught Tabix two strides past the post. The verdict was a short head in favour of his opponent.

His season, which had begun at Cheltenham in September, was not yet over. Eight months after that Cheltenham race, he contested the Church Fenton Handicap Hurdle at Wetherby and it was a surprising choice of race. The next day at Carlisle there was a similar event run over three miles and hundred yards in which Tabix carried a 6 lb. penalty. Red Rum's Perth run suggested that long distances such as that were what he needed, yet the Wetherby race was over two miles only. It was Red Rum's thirteenth of the season and for him thirteen was unlucky.

There were twenty-one runners and the pace, on firm ground, was a fast one. Red Rum, still adorned with blinkers, held a reasonable place for the first circuit and was not far behind the leaders when he made the first mistake of his jumping career. 'I don't think he quite fell; I more or less fell off him,' says Tommy Stack. 'He was down on his knees but he didn't roll over.' Sandra Kendall thinks Red Rum may have struck the heels of a horse in front as he prepared to take the second-last flight. Anyway, Red Rum quickly was up and cantering on, none the worse for his mishap. Sandra caught him without difficulty and back at Oxclose his appetite was as keen as ever.

'That was the thing about him : he always fought back. Whatever they did to him, he never got sickened and all through that long season he remained the same kind horse in his box though he really wasn't right in himself,' says Sandra.

Race fourteen was at Ayr on May 18, twelve days before the end of the season. The distance three miles and just one of the nine runners carried more weight than Red Rum. That horse, Tipperty, had begun his season in March and was having only his fifth outing. He ran well to finish second. Red Rum ran badly, never escaping from a poor position and passing the post almost twenty lengths behind the winner.

'A lot of the hope felt about the horse had been lost,' states Tommy Stack. He believed that Red Rum's repeated failures were attributable in part of his running in 'an awful lot of races' and to the after-effects of the cough. He also thought that Red Rum's attitude to racing left something to be desired.

Robert Renton, looking back, is philosophical about that barren season. 'I was never disappointed in the horse. During that second season over hurdles I was already thinking about his going over fences. I always said to Mrs Brotherton : "This is a National horse." '

But he, too, was not entirely satisfied with Red Rum's approach to racing. 'I fitted him with blinkers because Tommy thought he was running his races in snatches and wasn't going through with it. I thought the blinkers would sharpen him up.'

When he turned Red Rum out to grass in the summer of 1970, Robert Renton had made up his mind that Red Rum had run in his last hurdle race. He had been bought as a potential chaser and that would be his true métier. The fact that he had won three times as a first-season hurdler was a useful bonus.

Sandra Kendall continued to make her daily visits to Red Rum in the Oxclose paddock, with her bucket of corn, and was delighted to note that her favourite was doing far better physically than he had done the previous summer. Her faith in his ability as a racehorse was unshaken, as was her faith in his willing character.

The task of getting him fit once he had returned to the full stable routine was hers, for her employer fully recognised that she got on well with Red Rum. And, truth to tell, it is doubtful if any of the other stablelads would have relished the prospect of riding the bucking, skipping, prancing five-year-old down to the gallops.

The Renton novices were introduced to easy fences after their hurdling days, as a preliminary to schooling over some of regulation size, and Sandra thrilled to Red Rum's brilliance as a jumper. Tommy Stack did not share her sense of delight. He very rarely rode Red Rum at home and when he put him at one of the practice fences, Red Rum dug in his toes.

'It was very heavy going and no horse could have pulled out of it,' says Sandra, who watched that particular school. 'The next day I rode him – it had dried out, mind – and he jumped brilliantly. He never hesitated at all. I know Tommy won on him and knew him, but I don't think he ever really got on with Red Rum.'

In fact, Tommy did not feel any wild enthusiasm about partnering Red Rum in the Vittoria Novices' Chase at Newcastle on October 28, 1970, which was to be his first outing over fences. Newcastle's fences are fair and the course is an excellent one, but the fences are stiff and they can cause trouble to even an experienced chaser.

'He was a bit duck-hearted at home and I didn't think he would get round,' is Tommy's frank comment. Rare Comedy, who had done so much better over hurdles than Red Rum in the previous season, also was making his début over fences in the same race and he was well fancied, starting at 11 to 4. Red Rum, backward in appearance and known not to have done much work at home, was at 7 to 1. There were two virtually unconsidered outsiders, Royal Eden and Bright Imitation.

There was a surprise in store for Tommy at the first fence, for Red Rum judged it well and jumped it perfectly. 'His jumping was brilliant all the way,' He explains. So brilliant, in fact, that despite being some way short of peak fitness he was able to lie up with the leaders, Royal Eden, Mr Owen and Autumn Wood, the favourite. Rare Comedy came from the back to pass him before the second last and Paddy Broderick's special brand of determination took him to within a short head of Royal Eden on the line. Red Rum measured the last as accurately as he had the first and deprived Mr Owen of third place on the run-in.

Tommy had a new admiration for him, Sandra felt happier than she had done for a year and Robert Renton was well pleased with a run which promised much for the future.

The trainer, now turned eighty, had only just discontinued his habit of having at least one ride in a hurdle race every season. It was twenty years earlier that he had achieved the ambition of all National Hunt trainers and won the Grand National, with Freebooter, a horse he also had handled in his novice days. He had bought Freebooter on behalf of Mrs Brotherton for 3,000 guineas as a five-year-old and Freebooter's form had been so good before he went to Aintree for the 1970 Grand National that he was allotted 11 st. 11 lb. His victories had included the now defunct Champion Chase and the Grand Sefton at Liverpool.

He was nine years old when he first ran in the National and in his prime. A desperate blunder at the Chair threw Jimmy Power, a first-rate Aintree jockey, so far forward that his chest was on Freebooter's ears but miraculously Power regained the saddle and Freebooter scarcely checked in his stride. His leap at Becher's second time round was breathtaking and he joined Cloncarrig in the lead at the second last. Cloncarrig fell and Freebooter galloped on relentlessly to a victory which was as deserved as it was satisfying to those who loved to see a really good chaser win chasing's major prize.

Freebooter ran in two more Grand Nationals under top weight of 12 st. 7 lb., an impost which Red Rum would never have to carry, and finished in neither. He was brought down at the second fence in 1951 and fell at the Canal Turn on the second circuit in 1952 when disputing the lead with the eventual winner, Teal. 'A very, very bold horse. When he saw a fence he would pull you into it,' Robert Renton remembers. 'Red Rum, by contrast, was a very careful jumper. That is why he was the sort of horse who would jump the National fences, though I could not imagine Red Rum's becoming as good a National horse as Freebooter.'

The comparison became more pertinent in later years. At

that time, Red Rum had a long way to go to be worthy of any such flattery though he took a giant stride on his next outing at Doncaster, a course similar to Newcastle in providing a wonderfully fair, galloping track and fences which do not allow horses to take liberties. The event was the Town Moor Novices' Chase, worth £580 to the winner, and it was thought to be a formality for Orient War, a winner at Ayr and Haydock Park and trained by Arthur Stephenson at Bishop Auckland. Despite the promise of his Newcastle run, Red Rum was at 100 to 7.

The blinkers had been left off at Newcastle and they stayed off for Doncaster. Once again, Tommy had the ride and once again he let Red Rum bowl along near the leaders, a position he was able to maintain with not much expenditure of effort for his jumping was flawless. When Orient War made an error at the last fence on the first circuit, one of the most troublesome at Doncaster though just a plain fence, Red Rum took a couple of lengths off him. And after Oliver's Mount and Treble Kay had fallen Red Rum was asked by Tommy to go past Orient War when they had landed over the second from home. Red Rum answered well, took the last still in front and had enough in reserve to quicken on the flat. Orient War, having been outjumped by Red Rum at the last two, fought back to get to his quarters but could make no further progress.

'It was quite a surprise but then he had jumped well at Newcastle and we thought he was coming back to what we thought of him originally,' Tommy says. Mrs Brotherton had kind words for Red Rum and Robert Renton decided to send him down to Cheltenham yet again to take on two young stars, Jabeg and Soloning. He wouldn't be a rank outsider this time.

CHAPTER SIX

Cheltenham on November 13, 1970, was a pleasant place to be. The weather was fine and the ground was near perfect for racing. Red Rum had remained reasonably calm on the journey from Ripon and in his racecourse stable, so that hopes were high that he would give a good account of himself in the Borough Chase against Soloning, a hot favourite despite his not having had a previous race that season, and Jabeg, a highly-regarded five-year-old trained by Bob Turnell.

Jabeg had won a £2,000 novice chase at Newbury earlier in the month and he more than lived up to expectations by making all the running at Cheltenham. Soloning's jumping contained too many blemishes to enable him to match strides with Jabeg and he kept Red Rum out of second place by only half a length. Considering the class of the opposition, Red Rum had acquitted himself well. And he did so again when he went for a Wills Premier Chase qualifier at Wetherby exactly a week later.

The general impression of his Doncaster race had been that Orient War was beaten primarily because of his indifferent jumping, so although he met Red Rum on 1 lb. worse terms at Wetherby he started second favourite to his stable-companion, Huperade, who had won handicaps at Kelso and Doncaster on his two previous outings. Red Rum was also less fancied in the betting than Supermaster and Rare Comedy. Tony Gillam, later to have charge of Red Rum, claimed the 7 lb. allowance on Woodbridge, a mare trained at Wetherby by Tony Doyle.

Wetherby's fences are fair but formidable. Many jockeys prefer riding over them to the smaller, softer fences of courses such as Sedgefield, for if a horse can jump he will find things in his favour. The fences are well sited on good, flat land. Some novices, however, find them punishing when mistake are made and this was evident in that particular Wills qualifier. Seven of the twelve runners failed to finish.

With the final line of four fences left, Huperade held a narrow lead over Orient War. Red Rum was at their heels and Rare Comedy was beginning to fall away towards the backmarker, Woodbridge. At the third from home, Red Rum was about three lengths behind the two Arthur Stephenson horses and he held them to that margin as Huperade fought back and beat Orient War by a neck. 'He ran really well. They were two very good horses at the time,' says Tommy Stack.

A fortnight later, Robert Renton sent Red Rum to Sedgefield in County Durham for a three-mile conditions chase. Royal Eden, who had beaten him on his chasing debut at Newcastle, and Autumn Wood, who had been favourite for that same race, challenged him for the £272 first prize and Autumn Wood was seen as the most probable danger to him. Royal Eden was the 20 to 1 outsider of the six runners. Red Rum coped well with the little fences but the sharp, undulating track was far from ideal for him and he had to be hard ridden on the long run-in to catch Choir Belle, a moderate six-year-old.

Red Rum's sixth race within two months was the valuable Rowland Meyrick Chase at Wetherby on Boxing Day. In it he opposed three horses set to carry 5 lb. penalties, as he was, but whereas his had been incurred in that minor event at Sedgefield they had won handicaps. Favourite was Excess, trained at Newmarket by Tom Jones, a regular raider at the Yorkshire course, and ridden by Stan Mellor. Excess was unbeaten in two runs, at Warwick and Sandown. Red Rum's form scarcely matched up to that and he was at 10 to 1. Not for the first time in his career, he was the youngest horse in the field.

'I suppose he was doing plenty for a five-year-old but he was a tough sort of horse; you could never get to the bottom of him. He was as hard as nails,' states Tommy, who had a bad fall in a player's Hurdle Championship qualifier half an hour before he was due to partner Red Rum and, as a result, had to miss the ride. Macer Gifford deputised again. 'He ran well enough,' Tommy adds.

Kilmogany Five, one of the winners, made the running until halfway where Stan Mellor sent Excess on. Red Rum held him until into the last of the three miles but was fighting a losing battle from then on and would have been fourth not third had not Another Guy fallen when in the lead at the last. Excess was left clear and passed the post fourteen lengths ahead of Red Rum. The ground was yielding and in the circumstances Red Rum had satisfied his connections. There was not any suggestion this time that his inability to stay with the leaders had been mental rather than physical and the blinkers were still absent when he was sent up to Ayr in early February for the Girvan Handicap Chase.

'Mr Renton did not go racing much at that time,' says Sandra Kendall. 'My brother and I used to take Red Rum. He was responsible for declaring the horse to run; my job was to prepare Red Rum for the race.' By now, Red Rum was getting used to the long haul to Ayr and the racecourse surroundings were familiar to him. He was very much at peace with the world as he went to the start that day and there was stable confidence in him.

Brian Fletcher rode the top weight, Corseal, an Irish gelding who had newly arrived at Denys Smith's yard. He had won a minor novices' chase at Gowran Park but would have been way down the handicap if accurately assessed on his form. Banderole, with 12 st. 1 lb., was the true top of the handicap, a position he had earned with victories at Teesside and Wetherby. He was set to concede 9 lb. to Red Rum and Frank Carr's consistent Swan-Shot, an easy winner the previous month at Uttoxeter, had 5 lb. more than Red Rum. Both were preferred to him in the betting.

Tommy Stack's Wetherby fall had kept him out of the saddle for only a day and he had struck a good seam of winners. The distance of two and half miles suited some of the others more than it did Red Rum and he had to be ridden along to stay near the front. Banderole led at the third last, was joined in the lead by Red Rum at the last and was ousted by him on the flat. When he returned to the unsaddling enclosure he was lame and he did not race again that season so, possibly, he was an unlucky loser. Red Rum, however, had done all he had to do and his rehabilitation seemed complete.

It was very late on Friday, February 5, that Sandra and Kendall arrived back at Oxclose from Ayr with Red Rum. And it was early the following Friday that the three set off for another taxing journey in the opposite direction. This time the destination was Sandown and the objective the three-mile Compton Chase in which he shared top weight with Bill Shand-Kydd's top-class hunter-chaser, Rome Express; Even Delight, three times a winner earlier in the season; and Jask, successful earlier in chases at Nottingham and Newbury.

'I thought he was a certainty that day,' recalls Tommy. The betting reflected a certain confidence, too, and Red Rum started favourite at 7 to 2, a point less than Rome Express and Jask Lucky Edgar, third at Lingfield in his previous race, was nicely backed from 7 to 1 to 11 to 2 and as he was set to receive a stone from the three top weights because he had not won a race was thought likely to bustle them up.

Robert Renton was not at the meeting. Had he been, Sandra would have tried to persuade him to withdraw Red Rum. As it was, her brother did not have the authority to make such a decision and against their better judgment they saddled up Red Rum and Sandra led him round the parade ring with the other six runners.

Even before the starter dropped his flag Tommy knew that something was amise. 'He sweated up so much at the start that it was dripping off him. He usually got a bit hot but nothing like that. He was all of a jitter.' His forebodings were quickly confirmed when the starter sent them on their way. 'He never raised a gallop and never jumped a fence properly. He was a really good, careful jumper, light on his feet, but that day he hardly rose at any of them.'

The consequence was that Red Rum was tailed off before the second mile had been covered. Four horses completed the course, headed by Lucky Edgar. Red Rum was last of the four, some thirty lengths behind the winner.

'I have often thought since then that he was got at,' Tommy declares.

Sandra also is emphatic that Red Rum was not his normal

self. 'The horse was not right. I know Tommy thinks he might have been doped and that could have been it. But maybe the long journey from Ayr to home and then from home to Sandown was to blame. It had taken a lot out of him.'

Whatever the reason for his failure, Red Rum was not given much time to regain his strength and seemed not to need it. Less than a fortnight had elapsed since Sandown when he was driven up to Teesside Park for the Facey Romford Chase, a minor event carrying a total of £470 in prizemoney. He had seemed to be back to normal but evidently was not, for he was shaken off easily by Supermaster and Gyleburn in the straight.

Mrs Brotherton liked to have a runner at the Cheltenham Festival meeting and so Red Rum was earmarked for it in mid-March. His race was to be the Mildmay of Flete Challenge Cup Handicap Chase over two and a half miles. The meeting opened with ground officially described as dead and the first-day winners included the Australian star, Crisp, who took the National Hunt Two-Mile Champion Chase by twenty-five lengths. If anyone had suggested then to Fred Winter that he would be running Crisp two seasons later in the Grand National he would have dismissed the suggestion as ridiculous.

By the Wednesday, rain had made the ground decidedly soft and Bula deprived Persian War of his Champion Hurdle crown. By the Thursday the going on the chase course was so heavy that racing was doubtful for a time. Although the rain had washed away all hope in Red Rum, he still ran in the Mildmay and Tommy thought he did well 'to be just touched off for third place'. Not that Red Rum ever looked likely to win : the first two home were separated from the rest by a twenty-length gap.

Red Rum was to have three more races that season, making a total of thirteen and thirty-seven overall in the three seasons in which he had been trained by Robert Renton. At Wetherby on Easter Monday, he came back to two and a half miles and found himself outpaced by a local horse, Clear Cut, who three seasons later was to score a convincing victory in the Topham Trophy at Liverpool. Clear Cut had begun his racing career in Yorkshire point-to-point races, had been up for sale and then had been retained by his owner. He developed into an outstanding chaser with Charlie Hall at Tadcaster and reached a double-figure total of victories at Wetherby in his Topham year.

Red Rum was trying to concede 6 lb. to him at the Easter meeting. He was lower down the handicap when he returned to Wetherby for the Whitsuntide meeting and this time lost third place by two heads. Finally, at the very fag-end of the season, he was sent up to Perth and finished third of four to the moderate Mr Owen. There were scarcely any other meetings left when he went out of training for his summer rest.

When Red Rum went into temporary retirement in the June of 1971 his trainer, Robert Renton who was then 84 years old, chose to retire permanently. He retained ownership of Oxclose and decided to lease the stables, paddocks and gallops. His association with Tommy Stack as amateur and professional had been a happy one and he offered to let Tommy take over the premises and the horses in his care, subject of course to the approval of the owners.

Tommy was grateful for the offer and so began what was to be a very short career as a trainer. He started out the 1971–72 season with a dozen horses, including Red Rum, and he followed Robert Renton's example in entrusting all Red Rum's preliminary work at home to Sandra Kendall. He was to continue as a jockey, as well as training, and when he declared Red Rum for his first race of the new season, at Southwell on October 11, he told the Press Association that he would be riding him.

He was not expecting great things from the six-year-old gelding. 'I looked upon him as an average sort of handicapper who might be good enough to win a couple of races a season,' Tommy says. No schooling was given to Red Rum before that Southwell outing and Tommy knew that he would need a race or two to bring him to his peak. Consequently, Red Rum started at 16 to 1 for the three-mile Colonel R. Thompson Memorial Trophy Chase in which he was set to receive a stone from the top weight, The Inventor, a Ludlow winner four days earlier. Red Rum finished in front of The Inventor but a considerable way behind Nom de Guerre, trained by David Nicholson, another man who combined training with riding.

Red Rum was straighter in condition when he was sent to Kelso, just over the Scottish border, to contest another £1,000 chase over three miles twelve days later, yet he ran without sparkle. Red Sweeney, an intended Grand National entrant, and Slave's Dream, ridden by Brian Fletcher, fought a stern battle which was won by Red Sweeney. Red Rum was too far behind for Tommy to have any hope of reaching a place and he passed the line in fifth position.

It was by no means a satisfactory performance to Tommy and he brought back the blinkers for Red Rum's next outing, at Newcastle a fortnight later.

Irish Rain, third in the Kelso race on what was his first appearance of the season, was favourite this time. Slave's Dream, again ridden by Brian, was second favourite and in a field of seven runners Red Rum was one of three quoted at 16 to 1. Slave's Dream, jumping immaculately, led all the way but Red Rum left the remainder well behind as he went in pursuit on the final circuit and was only four lengths adrift at the post. Tommy felt the horse was recovering his form.

On the Sunday before that Newcastle race, Tommy had given up as a trainer. 'With the amount of travelling needed in racing over here, you can't be a success both as a trainer and a jockey,' he states. He had many years left to him as a jockey and chose to continue in that role.

Anthony Gillam, grandson of the late Major Lionel Holiday – (one of the most successful thoroughbred breeders in the history of British racing) – took over from him. 'I applied for the job and was lucky enough to get it.' Tony Gillam had ridden in point-to-points and hunter chases and had trained winners under permit. His horses always looked well and he rode stylishly and with quiet efficiency. He did not, however, ride Red Rum either on the racecourse or at home. Tommy continued to act as stable jockey and Sandra Kendall, he decided, got on so well with Red Rum that it was not worth considering any variation to the routine followed by Robert Renton and Tommy Stack.

It was about this time that Sandra Kendall sustained a broken collar bone while schooling another of the horses in the string, Naughty Story, on Ripon racecourse. She was off work for five weeks and Red Rum was handed over to a lad to look after. She looks back on that period as one of the blackest in all her time as a stablegirl.

'When I went back, Mr Renton was going to pull Red Rum out of training because he looked so bad. I nearly left through it, anyway. But I took Red Rum over again and began to coddle him back,' Sandra recalls.

An indifferent display followed in the Sundew Handicap Chase at Haydock in which he took on Red Sweeney and Nom de Guerre again. Blinkers were on Red Rum and it was generally assumed that he was not at his best; he drifted out to 10 to 1 in the betting. Though he had been allotted only 1 lb. above the minimum weight, he was left behind by the leaders in the final mile.

By the time that another ten days had elapsed, Sandra's devotion and hard work had brought about an astonishing revival in Red Rum. Tony Gillam was well pleased with his progress and took him to nearby Catterick Bridge for the Charles Vickery Memorial Handicap Chase, one of the most valuable chases run over the North Yorkshire course. Fortune Bay II, a seven-year-old of exceptional promise from the Arthur Stephenson stable was the even-money favourite, with Red Rum next at 9 to 2.

Tommy's advice to Tony Gillam was that the blinkers should stay on Red Rum for the time being, and his advice was accepted. The going was firm, which strengthened the hopes that Red Rum would run well, and Tommy was in top form, celebrating, it seemed, his release from the anxiety of training racehorses. He won the Hurworth Novices Chase, the second race on the card, and a division of a novices' hurdle, the third, for Tommy Shedden, the Wetherby trainer. Red Rum was the horse which could complete the hat-trick.

He did, and Tommy thinks that he may have had luck on his side. 'Fortune Bay looked dangerous when he unseated John Enright at the fourteenth.' Red Rum took over the lead three fences from home and gamely resisted the strong run of Proud King by a length. 'He won quite well,' says Tommy. It was a workmanlike performance not a brilliant one.

The feeling that Fortune Bay's mistake prevented Red Rum from finishing second was widely held by those who had seen the race and when they met again, over the same course and distance eleven days afterwards, Fortune Bay was at odds on. In the interim he had gained an easy success at Kelso, incurring a 6 lb. penalty. As a consequence, he had to concede 3 lb, to Red Rum, whereas he had been in receipt of 1 lb. in the Charles Vickery. Nom de Guerre, meeting Red Rum on the same terms as when he beat him at Haydock, divided Fortune Bay and Red Rum in the betting and, as it turned out, in the race.

Nom de Guerre and Golden Crisp, an unconsidered outsider, made the running together until David Nicholson sent on Nom de Guerre on the turn for home. Tommy had Red Rum at his heels and approaching the final fence there was little between them. John Enright, however, had been biding his time on Fortune Bay and he swept past both of them to win by five lengths. Tommy's assessment that Red Rum was an average handicapper capable of winning two or three chases a year – with a bit of luck – seemed to be an accurate one.

CHAPTER SEVEN

Red Rum's seventh race of the season and his first as a seven-year-old again was at Catterick, on New Year's Day, 1972. He carried a 6 lb. penalty for his December course and distance victory in the Zetland Handicap Chase and had three opponents. There was a little money for Permit, a horse who never did justify the five-figure sum paid for him after a fairly good but far from brilliant point-to-point career, and Kippie Lodge but the hot favourite was Mr Clifford Nicholson's Great Noise. This little horse had made all the running to win the Rowland Meyrick Chase at Wetherby on Boxing Day. He was a quick jumper and a talented racehorse but his legs told the tale about training difficulties.

Pat McCarron settled Great Noise behind Kippie Lodge and sent him on at the start of the third and final circuit. Red Rum, who had been urged along by Tommy Stack from halfway, caught him at the second last and drew away as Great Noise capitulated with surprising suddenness. It transpired that Great Noise had broken down again. He was to win a race the next season and to go to Aintree. Not for him, though, the fairy-tale happenings which were to befall Red Rum.

Tony Gillam considered Red Rum now deserved a rest and he planned a spring campaign for him. When Red Rum achieved that second Catterick victory, his trainer already had the Topham Trophy at the Grand National meeting in mind for him. 'We fancied a cut at the Topham because he was such a good jumper,' he recalls. The English climate is such that it

55

pays trainers to have alternatives prepared, especially when they are dealing with top-of-the-ground performers, and the alternative to the Topham was the Scottish Grand National at Ayr in April.

His preliminary run was to be at Catterick once more. There, on March 6, he started at odds on for the first time in his career though the going was yielding. He had five opponents, Best View – on whom Paddy Broderick had won the Gordon Foster Chase at Wetherby in October but who had been off the course since a failure later that month – the moderate Turmo-Tang and three just out of the novice stage. No wonder Red Rum was at odds on.

David French, one of the virtual novices, made the early running for Dennis Atkins and then gave way to Turmo-Tang. Passing the small stands for the second time Turmo-Tang began to struggle and David French went on again, tracked by Red Rum. Round the tight paddock bend, over a small plain fence and on to the open ditch with David French in front on the inside. Best View, ridden by David Goulding later to join Tony Gillam's stable, was close up on his outside and Tommy Stack still was tracking David French on Red Rum. Best View was going well enough to suggest that he would have a fight on his hands but the fight did not materialise. David French's lack of experience found him out at the ditch and down he went. Red Rum ran into him a stride after landing and over he went, too. Gone was one of the safest young chasers in training and his trainer's plan to introduce him to the Aintree fences. Fortunately, Red Rum was none the worse for the crash and after he had jumped around riderless Sandra Kendall caught him. He was not even scratched and, back home, ate heartily.

If is, perhaps, the biggest word in the English language. Certainly it towers over the lives and careers of men and women who follow pursuits in which chance is a dominant factor. Here are a few examples which spring to mind as a result of Red Rum's Catterick accident:

IF Red Rum had not been diverted from Liverpool would he have shown the aptitude for jumping those huge fences which Tony Gillam was sure he possessed and which was to become so brilliantly demonstrated the next season?

IF he had run well in the Topham, would his owner have

chosen him as the horse she could do without or would he have
revived memories of the great Freebooter to such an extent that,
winter sport or no winter sport, she would have sustained her
interest in steeplechasing just a little longer?

IF Red Rum had stayed at Ripon would Brian Fletcher have
gained the recognition and great success which his fight back
from serious injury so justly deserved and which was the
motivating factor behind his decision to carry on as a jockey?

The answers to those three questions, on the balance of
probability are Yes, Yes and No. But Red Rum did not go for
the Topham and Tony Gillam had sound reasons for switching
his attack to the Scottish Grand National.

'The Topham would have been his next run after being
brought down and it looked like being a soft Liverpool. In
those circumstances it didn't seem a sensible step to take.' He
fully recognised that Red Rum needed long distances but he
chose the two-and-three-quarter-mile Trent Handicap Chase at
Nottingham in late March as the confidence-restorer for Red
Rum, hoping for sound going. In fact, heavy rain softened the
ground and he was not unduly disappointed when Red Rum
was beaten into third place by David Nicholson's consistent
Nom de Guerre and the little-fancied Guiburn.

Macer Gifford, brother of Josh, rode Red Rum at Notting-
ham. Tommy Stack replaced him at Wetherby on Easter
Monday when he was one of five runners for the £3,000
Wetherby Handicap Chase, the most valuable chase at any of
the plethora of jumping meetings that day. The opposition was
hot this time. Ballysagert had finished in front of Charlie
Potheen and the Irish crack, Sea Brief, when second to Clever
Scot in the Totalisator Champion Chase at the Cheltenham
Festival meeting and Jomon, trained at Newmarket by Tom
Jones, had won the National Hunt Handicap Chase 35 minutes
later. The ground at Cheltenham was soft, as it was at Wetherby
that Easter Monday, and they both were demonstrably at their
most effective on it.

Supermaster, the top weight, had been favourite for the
National Hunt Chase on the strength of his second place to
Young Ash Leaf in the Greenall Whitley Chase at Haydock in
March and had a superb record at Wetherby. Only Petruchio's
Son, who had lost the form which had brought him five suc-

cessive victories in the early weeks of the season, was weaker in the betting market than Red Rum. He was at 20 to 1; Red Rum was offered at 10 to 1, though starting at a point less, and the bulk of the money was for Jomon and Ballysagert, in that order.

Red Rum, bottom of the handicap by 9 lb. and receiving 25 lb. from Supermaster, tracked Petruchio's Son until the eleventh fence and then went into the lead on the last circuit. Supermaster hit the open ditch hard and began to drop behind as John Enright brought Ballysagert into closer touch and Stan Mellor pushed Jomon almost alongside Red Rum as they started on the bed into the straight for the last time. Ballysagert went past them as they approached the open ditch, four from home, and Jomon took second place.

Both were noted for stamina, both acted well on the soft ground and both could have been expected to pull right away from Red Rum. They did not. Hard ridden by Tommy Stack, he refused to be shaken off and although the real battle from the last concerned the other two he was beaten only three and a half lengths by Ballysagert and a mere one and a half by Jomon. The form was very near to his best. Tony Gillam maintains: 'He just couldn't go as well in soft ground as he could on firm.' The formbook does not bear this out.

The Scottish Grand National was 12 days later and by then a fine spell of weather had brought the Ayr going to good. Tommy Stack had been riding regularly for Ken Oliver, the Hawick trainer, who had asked him to ride Young Ash Leaf in all her races. Young Ash Lead was a potentially top-class but erratic chaser and had run the best race of her career when ridden by Tommy in the Greenall Whitley at Haydock, giving 8 lb. and a two-and-a-half-length beating to Supermaster. And his trainer regarded her highly enough to run her later in the Cheltenham Gold Cup.

'I thought the mare would run well and, quite honestly, I didn't fancy the chance of Red Rum,' states Tommy.

Because Tony Gillam was certain that Red Rum was a horse who needed knowing, he engaged Macer Gifford even though he would have had to put up 7 lb. overwight – Red Rum was one of the three runners sharing bottom weight of 9 st. 7 lb. A staff strike at Heathrow Airport foiled that plan and at the

Above: Red Rum (Tommy
Stack), in the colours of Mrs
Lurline Brotherton, leads Proud
Knight over the last to win the
Charles Vickery Memorial Chase
at Catterick in December 1971
Right: Sandra Kendall, delighted
by Red Rum's return to fitness
and form, leads him in after the
Charles Vickery at Catterick

Above: Red Rum
reaching for a fence
during the Salamanca
Handicap Chase at
Newcastle, his third
race for Donald McCain
Left: Red Rum, a
picture of health, after
the Salamanca

Donald McCain – forthright, frank, modest, optimistic and Red Rum's fervent admirer

Above: Crisp is away in front as Brian Fletcher steers a careful course at the Chair fence in the 1973 National. Great Noise is in a bit of trouble on his left, alongside Rouge Autumn, Sunny Lad and, in the spots, Black Secret

Below: Red Rum chasing hard at the last has Crisp in view after a full circuit of stamina-sapping pursuit. 'I had seen Crisp's old tail go round and I knew he was tiring,' Brian states

An exhausted Crisp finds the post just too far away and Red Rum catches him in the last strides

Above: Red Rum on his way to the start of the Greenall Whitley
Chase at Haydock in March 1974. He lost his jockey, through no fault
of his own or Brian's, after the first fence and yet ran an excellent
Grand National trial

Below: Red Rum in his customary sheepskin noseband, puts all his
effort into his final National work-out along the Southport beach,
accompanied by Glenkiln

Above: Red Rum in the stable of trainer Donald McCain
Below: Red Rum on the sands at Southport. Donald McCain is on the
left, flanking Red Rum are The Tunku (left) and Glenkiln

Red Rum leads L'Escargot in the Grand National parade flanked by his head lad, Jackie Grainger, and stable lad, Billy Ellison

Above: Red Rum, full of eagerness, on his way to the start of the 1974
Grand National
Below: Red Rum jumps into the lead at Becher's second time round
in the 1974 National. Charles Dickens is close behind

Above: Red Rum (in the lead) clears Becher's Brook for the last time in the 1974 Grand National
Below: Red Rum, still full of running, leads a tired L'Escargot over the last in the 1974 Grand National. Within another hundred yards he had made sure of victory

Red Rum, ears pricked and still going powerfully, wins the Grand National for the second time

Above: Mrs Beryl McCain greets Red Rum, who is being led in by Billy Ellison and Jackie Grainger, the head lad. In two seasons with Red Rum, Billy became the richer by £2,800 excluding his wages. He wagered very heavily by a stablelad's standards on Red Rum and was able to say at the end of the 1973–74 season that his beloved horse had won a house for him. Sandra Kendall, Billy's predecessor, also backed Red Rum in both his Grand Nationals though modestly. She did not back him at all while she was 'doing' him. 'I thought it might bring bad luck,' she says

Below: Wearing his Blue Riband for the second time in two years, Red Rum is led back by Billy Ellison to the racecourse stables

Red Rum is rewarded by Donald McCain's wife after winning the
1974 Grand National

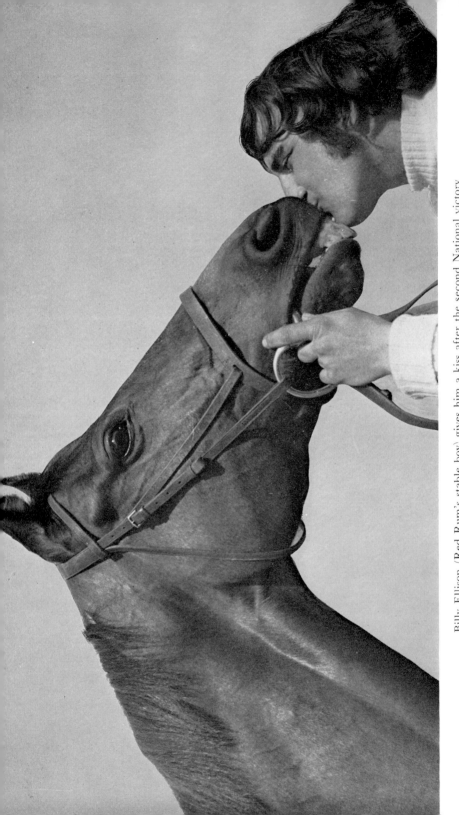

Billy Ellison (Red Rum's stable boy) gives him a kiss after the second National victory

An amalgam of pleasure and relief on the face of Donald McCain as
he stands alongside Red Rum in the Ayr winner's enclosure

Red Rum

time that jockeys were declared for the Scottish National Macer Gifford was grounded at Heathrow. Although Paddy Broderick had ridden Polar Bear for Gillam in the earlier London and Norther Securities Future Champions Chase, he would have had to put up several pounds overweight and waiting in the wings was Martin Blackshaw.

Martin, son of Harry, the Middleham trainer, was at the meeting to ride Persian War for Henry Alper in the Scottish Champion Hurdle later in the day. A successful apprentice on the flat before increasing weight directed him to National Hunt racing, Martin is a stylish rider and strong in the finish. When Tony Gillam heard that Macer Gifford could not get to the meeting in time, he booked Martin. He weighed out at 9 st. 8 lb., as did the riders of the other bottom weights, Sir Roger and Black Justice.

'Martin deputised very ably,' says Tony Gillam. The trainer had never tied down Tommy Stack to orders on Red Rum – 'Good heavens, no. He knew the horse better than I did.' But he did have orders for Martin. 'Stay close and kick on from the top bend.' That bend comes before the third from home. In fact, things did not go according to plan.

Slave's Dream, an out-and-out stayer who had led almost throughout in the John Smith's Great Yorkshire Chase at Doncaster in the previous January, made the running with Red Rum in a leading group which also included Beggar's Way, Esban and The Spaniard. After jumping the nineteenth of the twenty-six fences, Martin Blackshaw decided that then was the time to kick on. 'That was at the bottom bend, not the top one,' Tony Gillam explains. 'By the time he had reached the point where I wanted him to go on, Red Rum had run his race out.'

Red Rum passed the post in fifth place, just over seven lengths behind Quick Reply whose rider lost his irons at the last yet contrived to keep him two lengths clear of Slave's Dream. Esban and Beggar's Way, the latter of whom had been second in the Irish Grand National on his previous outing, were third and fourth. Sound staying chasers of the quality of Ashville, Red Sweeney and Sir Roger were well behind Red Rum. Tommy Stack had brought Young Ash Leaf into a challenging position after halfway but had been without hope in the last mile. 'She needed firmer ground.'

Tony Gillam felt that if Red Rum had been ridden by a jockey who had known him he might just about have won. Sandra Kendall was more dogmatic. 'He sent him on fifteen to twenty lengths clear didn't he? What was he thinking of?' Tommy Stack, able to follow Red Rum's running at reasonably close quarters, thought the horse had run a great race. 'Far better than I thought he would. He wasn't beaten far.' As it was, Red Rum's performance was to be noted by a virtually unknown Southport trainer when he combed a sales catalogue later in the year and it was to influence him to make a decision which was to change his life dramatically. Tony Gillam, for his part, was more convinced than ever that Red Rum had no stamina limitations and that he was the type of horse to do well in the Grand National.

He would have liked to put his theory to the test but was not to get the opportunity to do so. Red Rum's days in his stable were numbered. He saddled him for the last time at Market Rasen a fortnight after the Scottish National. Tommy Stack had the ride and Red Rum started favourite for a three-mile handicap in which he carried 10 st. 4 lb. For two and a half miles he kept on terms with the leaders, then the effort began to tell and he weakened. Only one horse finished behind him, and that a blinkered eleven-year-old who started at 33 to 1. 'He had gone by then,' says Tony Gillam.

Red Rum was a seven-year-old, and a progressive one at that. He had shown that he was a careful and sure-footed chaser, that long distances suited him well and that he was as sound as a bell. His legs had never given the slightest cause for concern, his respiratory organs were perfect and, overall, he had the constitution of a composite Emile Zatopek and Emlyn Hughes. He was the type of horse which the National Hunt enthusiast would love to own but the sunshine in the summer of 1972 served only to emphasise to Mrs Lurline Brotherton that National Hunt racing is synonymous with rain and cold and harsh journeys.

It has been known for flat races to be held in conditions of discomfort to both competitor and owner. Still, an owner could pick and choose and the height of summer offers a much better prospect than the depth of an English winter. Accordingly, Mrs Brotherton's interest in National Hunt racing was waning. Perhaps, if her old friend Robert Renton had not retired she would have sustained that interest longer. She thinks that probably is true. 'Yet I was getting too old and I was finding the weather too cold,' she explained one lovely June evening in 1974 after watching a very promising two-year-old called Fretta carry her blue and silver halved colours to victory at Beverley.

Back in the summer of 1972 she had several young horses in training for the flat and she made a firm decision to cut down on her chasers. 'I still have National Hunt horses but usually they are my flat horses who have been put over hurdles as a preliminary to my selling them.' If Tony Gillam had had his way, Red Rum would not have been the one to depart. 'Mrs Brotherton had horses coming off the flat to go jumping and she wanted to make a cut somewhere. She chose Red Rum as the one to go,' he says. She retained Polar Bear, one year Red Rum's junior, who had won three hurdles races at Catterick in the 1970-1 season and had scored by fifteen lengths in a novice chase at Wetherby on the day that Red Rum ran third to Ballysagert. He was never to fulfil that promise and proved to be an erratic handicap chaser.

Although Sandra Kendall had been Red Rum's constant companion for more than four years, during which he had won eight times, she felt she was still a person seemingly of no importance to Mrs Brotherton. The eight victories had not made any impression on her earnings and she resented the fact that Red Rum's owner – in her judgment – paid little attention to him when things were not going well for him. When Red Rum was having hard races and being well beaten, Sandra gave him more care and attention not less, and she dearly would have liked him to have an owner who took her into her confidence, who was prepared to discuss her plans for the horse. Instead, the threat of Red Rum's being sold had been hanging over her during that second, desperately-trying year over hurdles and it had been disconcerting for her not to have any reassurance even when Red Rum had pulled himself off the floor, as it were, and made a reasonable success of his new career as a chaser.

Perhaps she should have realised that Red Rum's days in the ownership of Mrs Brotherton were numbered and prepared herself for the blow which was to come. Perhaps it was for the best that she put such thoughts to the back of her mind. In the event, she felt shattered when the news that Red Rum was to go to the Doncaster Sales was broken to her. 'I went mad; I could not believe it. I had one hell of a row with them. Then they wouldn't let me take him to the sales in case I brought the price down.' Instead, Sandra went on holiday the day that Red Rum was driven from Oxclose for the last time.

Tony Gillam, like Sandra, very much wanted to keep Red Rum in his stable and accompanied him to the Doncaster August Sales. The sales area, situated close by the magnificent new grandstand at the Yorkshire course, has recaptured much of its former atmosphere after the sales had been allowed to lapse. Now not only the St Leger Sales are held but also several other ones throughout the year. There were other good horses there with Red Rum but none caught the eye so much in the preliminary parade ring. As he made his way along the narrow gangway to the small ring immediately outside the covered sale-ring he was his usual exuberant self. Among those who took one last look before hurrying into the stands surrounding the ring was a tall Lancastrian who had a commission to buy a likely Grand National horse. He had paid particular attention to Red Rum's performance in the Scottish Grand National. 'It was obvious that he would stay the National distance and he was the right age,' he says.

The bidding was brisk and reached 6,000 guineas Tony Gillam helped it on its way – 'But I was beaten a bit before the end.' The final nod was made by that tall Lancastrian, Donald McCain, on behalf of an octogenarian whose interest in the Grand National went back to the start of the century. Tony Gillam returned to Oxclose regretting that he had lost a horse who one day might have run well for him in the Grand National; Donald McCain returned to his Southport home delighted that he had acquired a horse who might fulfil an ambition he had cradled since his boyhood days when he helped with hackneys at Lancashire shows.

'It sounds like being wise after the event, but we did genuinely think of Red Rum as a National horse, though in no way did I ever think he would reach the dizzy heights he has done,' Tony Gillam says two years later. 'I thought of him as a horse who by some stroke of magic might have won a Grand National; and it would have been great for me to have him placed third or fourth, something like that. I could never imagine him as a record-breaker. What he has become is quite fantastic and beyond anything I ever considered.'

Sandra voiced her opinions with conviction and a certain anguish. 'I told Mr Renton just before I want on holiday, "You are making the biggest mistake you could in selling him. He'll win next year's Grand National." But he told me I had always overrated Red Rum. I told Mrs Brotherton, too, but they said my motive was just to keep the horse. I knew he was a horse and a half and was getting better and better.' Robert Renton, who was Mrs Brotherton's adviser and friend as well as former trainer, maintains that he did, in fact, see Red Rum as a possible Grand National winner of the future. Mrs Brotherton, however, saw cold, wet months of winter racing ahead and did not share in any dreams of a second Liverpool triumph to add to that of Freebooter.

After her holiday and the departure of Red Rum, Sandra returned to work for Tony Gillam while the finishing touches were put to the house in Ripon to which she was to move after her impending marriage. When the house was ready, she married, became Mrs Miles and did not go racing again. She had enjoyed her life in racing and known excitement, joy and sadness.

'Dagmar was very close to me, and when they sold him it broke my heart – but I was young then.' But even Dagmar Gittell was not so deep in her affection as was Red Rum. 'I had eight ponies and two horses of my own at the time that I was looking after Red Rum and I hadn't a fraction of the interest in them that I had in him,' she says. Now happily married and with a baby daughter, she does not have any desire to go racing again but her interest in racing has survived through the horse she once rode. 'I always look to see where he is running and to see how he has done. And I'd love to go over and see him one day. That's the trouble, I suppose, with being a stablegirl – or a stableboy – you get to know your horse so well . . .'

CHAPTER EIGHT

Red Alligator's victory in the 1968 Grand National firmly established Brian Fletcher's reputation as a fine Aintree jockey and it has been retained over the years. It also lifted him on to the plateau to which all young jockeys aspire.

'I was on the way up before Red Alligator's win and ever since then I have been given the credit for being a good Aintree rider. In racing, you tend to get a certain number of good horses to ride and to get a certain number of winners. You hover for a time and either keep going on the same good level, if you get the horses to ride, or your total of winners begins to fall away. With my winning the National, I had a good year or two after it and I have kept going on the forty to fifty level. I have had the pleasure of having good horses to ride and of being able to do justice to them.

'I always thought of the National as the greatest race and as being capable of giving a steeplechase jockey the greatest thrill of his life, but I haven't any preference between steeplechasing and hurdling. I love to ride a good horse, no matter whether it is a steeplechaser or not. I think a jockey can be seen at his best on a good horse and at his worst on a bad one. It depends so much on the horse.'

He was off the mark quickly in the season after Red Alligator's triumph, scoring at Cheltenham for a Southern stable in a selling chase in September. The following month he began a profitable partnership with the four-year-old Most Handsome, trained by Denys Smith. On his first outing, Most Handsome won a novice hurdle easily at Wetherby and later in the season they won four successive chases together. He also gained an early-season win on Black Ice for the Wetherby trainer, Deryck Bastiman, at Uttoxeter and the following week achieved his first Ascot victory on the same horse.

Red Alligator's debut was delayed until the November, when he went to Cheltenham for a three-mile chase. His old rival, Bassnet, was favourite, while Red Alligator was little fancied. He trailed along at the back of the six-runner field throughout. Another two months passed by before he reappeared at Catterick and ran appallingly. The Grand National, which again was his target, was eight weeks away when Red Alligator tried to redeem his reputation in the Haydock Park National Trial. The handicapper had not relented and only Bassnet carried more weight.

From the moment the starter let them go, Red Alligator showed that some of his old zest was still with him and Brian was able to send him into the lead at the third last. Permit deprived him of it at the last but he rallied to beat him by half a length, though Game Purston pushed his nose in front on the line.

The racing public attached a lot more significance to that Haydock performance by Red Alligator than did his jockey, who feared that a third visit to Aintree would not meet with the horse's approval at all. Immediately, he shot to the head of the advance betting lists for the National and there he stayed. Despite a lot of money on the big day for Fearless Fred, a winner over the Haydock three and a half miles, Red Alligator was made favourite to repeat his victory of the previous year. He had 13 lb. more to carry.

There were 30 runners and once more Brian took Red Alligator towards the outside as they lined up. He jumped well enough but too deliberately and at the first Canal Turn had only five of the twenty-six survivors behind him. They included Moidore's Token, runner-up to him the year before. Brian found Red Alligator was unable to improve his position on the run towards the stands and was entirely without hope when the open ditch, three fences before Becher's, claimed him. Highland Wedding, also having his third attempt in the race, was well up with the leaders at that stage and eventually he ran on to a twelve-length victory.

65

Red Alligator apart, the season was a more than satisfactory one for the 21-year-old jockey. He was among the winners again by September in the following season, during which he was to ride forty-four winners. Surprisingly, Red Alligator won three times for him and seemed to enjoy a new lease of life. From the time that Red Alligator ran third in the Gordon Foster Chase at Wetherby, in early October, Brian knew that barring accidents he would have a fourth ride in the Grand National.

Red Alligator revived memories of his best year with a victory in the St Helen's Chase at Haydock, often a pointer to the National, but before National day came along he had twice failed dismally. The handicapper reduced his weight by one pound, compared with the previous year, and there was enough money for him to make him joint fourth favourite. Brian persuaded him to stay in closer touch to the leaders than in Highland Wedding's year and he was well placed when another open ditch put him on the ground, this time on the first circuit and two fences after Valentine's. There was to be no return visit for Red Alligator. Indeed, he had run in his last race.

Three Grand Nationals later, Brian was asked to compare the merit and the character of Red Alligator and his new hero. In regard to merit, he left that to the onlookers and the form experts. But he did not differentiate between them in one respect. 'Like Red Rum, Red Alligator was a very, very tough horse and very brave one.'

CHAPTER NINE

Liverpool, 1971, saw justice done by Specify in the Grand National at the expense of a gallant mare, Sandy Sprite, who had broken down and yet still led over the last. Specify had been going strongly at the second Becher's the year before when brought down by The Otter. Now he squeezed through a narrow gap on the rails after the elbow and beat Black Secret by a neck. Brian partnered a 20 to 1 shot, Inventor, for Eric Cousins. He was six places ahead of Specify at halfway and still in front of him at the second Canal Turn, but Inventor's stamina ran out soon afterwards and he refused at the ditch which had ended Red Alligator's challenge the year before.

Nevertheless, it was another good year for Brian and he reached his highest-ever total of winners – forty-six. Dondieu had gone well for him in the Champion Hurdle and later had won the Scottish Champion Hurdle in great style. Brian could look forward to the next Champion Hurdle with hope and not a little confidence even if there was no ready successor to Red Alligator in his circle of equine acquaintances.

As always, however, Denys Smith had some useful chasers in his stable despite the fact that he was turning his attention more and more to flat-racing and cutting back on the number of National Hunt horses. That's Life was one of them and he began the new season auspiciously with a win for Brian in a Wills Premier Chase qualifier at Ayr on an October Saturday. Two days later, over the same course, Dondieu carried 12 st. 7 lb. – 10 st. of it Brian Fletcher – into third place in a two-mile handicap hurdle, so confirming all the praise which had been heaped on him the season before.

That's Life won three more races for him and ran second to the Irish star, Colebridge, in the Wills final at Haydock. Doudieu followed his initial success by beating Baltus and Corrieghoil, two near top-class hurdlers, without having to be hard ridden in the £6,000 Fighting Fifth Hurdle at Newcastle. Odds of 11 to 4 were laid on him for his next race, at Wolverhampton, but he ricked his back and could finish only fourth to True Luck. More than three months passed before he was fit to race again and it came as very welcome reassurance for Brian and Denys Smith when Dondieu made virtually all the running in the City Trial Hurdle at Nottingham. He would, after all, be ready to tackle Bula again at Cheltenham.

It was to be an interesting and potentially profitable Cheltenham for Brian : there was Blank Check, an easy winner at Sedgefield, in the Totalisator Champion Chase; Chesapeake Bay, on whom he had won at Ayr, in the National Hunt Handicap Chase; That's Life in the Mildmay of Flete Challenge Cup; and Tartuffe who was to take on the Fred Winter ace, Pendil, in the Arkle Challenge Trophy Chase.

Blank Check and Tartuffe were taken to Teesside Park for their pre-Cheltenham races on February 23, 1972. Blank Check was well backed for the Facey Romford Handicap Chase in which he carried a 6 lb. penalty. Brian settled him in second place to Kippie Lodge, took him to the front at the twelfth and enjoyed an unexacting victory. A quick change into the Red Alligator colours and he was on board Sword Thrust for a two-mile handicap hurdle. That time he just missed third place. Ten minutes or so later he weighed out again for the Bilsdale Novices' Chase, worth £170 to the winner. That much he remembers.

CHAPTER TEN

'Tartuffe was a good horse at the time and was going out to win for the third time in succession,' says Brian. Three weeks beforehand Tartuffe had jumped beautifully for him at Ayr, where the fences are stiff, and had beaten the good youngster, The Chisler, in a two-mile novices' chase and a week before that he had won comfortably at Newcastle. Not surprisingly, he started at odds on in the Bilsdale Novices' Chase. All went well until the fifth fence. Brian has no recollection beyond what happened there. 'He absolutely buried me.'

He was taken to hospital and did not recover consciousness for ten days. 'When eventually I did come round I did not know where I was or what I was doing. I had also broken a bone in my arm and I wasn't aware of that. Even when I got home I really didn't know what I was doing.' His head had taken the brunt of a terrible fall and his brain had suffered a severe buffeting.

'I got myself pulled round and began the process of getting fit and then had to go to London for examination by a specialist to see if I was fit to resume riding. He had a look at me and told me that he wanted me to pack up riding. He said, "You have had a nasty fall, Brian, and I think you would be better off if you called it a day and got some insurance." ' Those words, uttered with the utmost tact, nevertheless were almost sickening in their impact.

Brian absorbed them and gave his reply. 'I'm sorry, Sir,' he told the specialist, 'I wouldn't know what to do with myself. I would prefer to give it more time and come back to see you in another two months or so. I want to carry on as a jockey.' Four months already had elapsed since the fall and he had to admit to himself that he was far from one hundred per cent. Two years later he is still suffering from the effects of that Teesside fall, and others. 'I used to feel on top of the world all the time, but now I get headaches and lots of other ailments due to concussion and I think to myself when I'm having a bad time, "You must have been a bloody fool to carry on." '

What made him pursue his fight to regain his jockey's licence and to embark again on a career in which danger is ever-present? 'I wanted to achieve something so that in the years to come I could look back and say to my children, "I did that or I was the only man to achieve this,' and I love the sport of National Hunt racing. When I cease to enjoy it and start to worry about what I'm doing when I'm riding I will pack up.'

Brian regards his wife's attitude to his injury and his decision to stay as a jockey if at all posssible as an immense contribution to his making a correct assessment of what his plans should be. 'While I was in the process of pulling myself round, my wife neither disheartened me nor encouraged me to continue as a jockey. This was a great asset. If someone had been in the background trying to influence me one way or the other it would have been a hindrance. Instead, I was left to make up my own mind. No one forced me to do anything.'

The young Brian Fletcher was not satisfied with one Grand National victory. It had been a great thrill to him to take part in any race, never mind the National, and he would never forget the wonderful, indescribable feeling which Red Alligator gave him as he pounded up the run-in at Liverpool but that was not enough on which to retire. 'I wanted to be able to look back on my career and say to myself that I really was good in my hey-day.'

So he gave up thoughts of accepting the compensation due to jockeys forced out of racing by injury. 'I had just moved into my farm, and I was hard up but if it wasn't for the love of the sport and the pleasure of doing it I would not have gone on.'

Not that he embarked on his rehabilitation with any reckless-ness. He was well aware of the risks entailed. 'When I started to ride out again, I always had it in the back of my mind that I would not have to overdo the job and that I would have to take things carefully for a while.' He rode out and he worked round the farm, and gradually he turned the corner. Two months after that first interview with the specialist, he was back in London for an examination which definitely would determine the course his life was to take. He felt optimistic and he was justified in doing so. The specialist gave him a clean bill of health.

He returned to his farm with his good news and planned his return to the racecourse. 'It was a great help being attached to a good stable like Denys's.' And he was especially grateful to a former jockey, Tommy Wyse, who was assistant to Denys Smith. Tommy helped Brian then as he had done before. 'A lot of the credit for whatever I have achieved must be put down to Tommy,' says Brian. 'He taught me virtually everything I know about racing, jumping-wise. I will always remember him and be grateful to him.' His understanding of Brian's problems in trying to find his feet again in National Hunt racing and the useful advice he gave to him were, Brian feels, of great benefit to him.

Other people in the sometimes harsh world of racing were less helpful. 'I was trying to get myself going and get the winners again, and I had to stick my neck out to try to get good rides. I won't mention any names, but the reply of some trainers was, "We'll see; I'll let you know." They thought I might not be quite right again and they were going to wait until they were sure I was before they put me up.' Loyalty was not their strongpoint.

Most jockeys have to face such a crisis in their careers at some time or other, and Brian readily admits that it is not possible to bounce back after a serious injury and immediately hit top riding form. 'I was a wee bit apprehensive for my first few rides,' he remembers.

The way back towards the top began on September 9 at Sedgefield, three weeks before Red Rum made his first appearance for his new stable. Brian's mount was Walshaw Demon, 20 to 1 in a field of eight for the Aycliffe Novices' Hurdle. It was the four-year-old's first attempt at hurdling and there could have been better ways of restoring confidence but, as Brian

says, he has always been prepared to have a go. Walshaw
Demon ran the kind of race his price indicated he would. He
was well behind the leaders in no time and stayed tailed off.
Brian dismounted, carried his saddle to the weighing room,
changed and made the short journey home. He was well pleased
with the day's work.

The weather was dry and the ground very firm, so that
opportunities to get rides were few and far between in those
early weeks of the season. It was into October when he got
another booking, this time back at Teesside Park. Denys Smith
put him up on Caley's Harvest, a five-year-old, in a £1,000
handicap hurdle. Caley's Harvest had won novice hurdles the
previous season and had scored on the flat. Though having his
first race of the new season, he was fit and started favourite.
He ran deplorably, being in the rear group throughout, while
the winner was another Denys Smith runner, Sword Thrust.
Starting at 12 to 1, Sword Thrust was the mount of Michael
Eddery.

Michael, brother of Pat – Peter Walwyn's talented flat jockey
– had become too heavy for flat-racing. He claimed the 7 lb.
allowance and was very good value for it, riding with dash and
style, but his was to be a short career. Not long afterwards he
smashed a leg when a hurdler crashed through the wing of a
Teesside obstacle and, tragically, the leg had to be amputated
below the knee. But as Sword Thrust was led into the winner's
enclosure the future looked bright for Michael and of an in-
determinate hue for Brian. Caley's Harvest was his only ride
of the day.

Two days later he was at Ayr to partner a couple of well-
fancied horses for Denys Smith. War Cry, a winner over the
course the previous season, looked to be well in at the weights
in the Punch Bowl Handicap Hurdle and Scorton Boy, a tough
gelding with a win on the flat at Edinburgh to his credit, had
jumped well at home and was thought sure to go well in a
three-year-old hurdle. Brian held up War Cry as Kelly Kos
was sent clear in the early stages of the Punch Bowl Hurdle.
Not until well past halfway did he make a move but it was in
good time. War Cry collared Kelly Kos at the second last and
raced away to a comfortable victory.

'Once I got the winner, the apprehension went out of my

mind completely,' states Brian. He felt the old confidence sweep back. Scorton Boy rounded off a momentous day by winning his hurdle race easily by eight lengths after being encouraged by Brian to stay in the front rank all the way.

Two days later again, Brian drove down the A1 to Wetherby where he was to ride another hurdler trained by Denys Smith, Moon Lady. She ran quite well in the Newton Handicap Hurdle and afterwards, as he changed, Ron Barry was preparing to weigh out to ride Red Rum in the Gordon Foster Handicap Chase. Ron was deputising for Tommy Stack, whose new retainer for Harry Thomson Jones had called him down to Cheltenham where he won a novice hurdle on Cannelloni. There was nothing to suggest to Brian at that time that he would ever have an intimate association with Red Rum.

'I didn't have a retainer with Denys Smith, just a mutual agreement that I should ride out his horses and ride for him in races. Denys had good horses and it was a well-run stable, and so I was lucky enough to get the chance to re-establish myself. If I had been riding bad horses I might have said to myself, "What the hell am I doing here." '

Other trainers began to book him again, among them Neville Crump who had his eye on Liverpool again. He had bought a Northern point-to-pointer, Canharis, for Lord Zetland. Canharis had been been known to run out in his point days and though he had made a successful first appearance over fences he was a difficult ride and a far-from-accurate jumper. Bold front-running was his hallmark.

Canharis was due to have his first run of the 1972–73 season at Newcastle in early November, in the three-mile John Eustace Smith Trophy Chase. The fact that Neville Crump engaged Brian as deputy for Pat Buckley was gratifying recognition to Brian that he really was back at the top, even though Canharis was not expected to trouble chasers of the calibre of Titus Oates and Ballysagert. In his last four races the previous season, Canharis had burst away in front only to weaken rapidly in the last half mile or so. Even moderate hunter-chasers had been leaving him well behind.

So when Brian bounced Canharis away in front at Newcastle, Ron Barry on Titus Oates was not unduly concerned and neither were the other four jockeys. When Canharis still held a good lead entering the last mile, Titus Oates was asked to reduce the gap but it was Canharis who had the greater reserves of energy and he pulled further away from the remainder in the straight to win by eight lengths, at 25 to 1. A few days after that, Donald McCain asked Brian if he would take over as Red Rum's regular jockey with a view to riding him in the Grand National. The most triumphant chapter in the young jockey's life, and in that of a great-hearted steeplechaser, was about to begin.

CHAPTER ELEVEN

When Donald McCain made that successful bid for Red Rum at Doncaster he was scarcely known by the racing public and little known to the racing press. He had become known to Mr Noel le Mare, the man who gave him the commission to buy him a Grand National horse, through his driving.

Donald McCain did not have a horsey background and, lacking that, did not get the opportunity to gain an active interest in ponies. 'I started straight off with horses, at round about the age of fourteen. I used to go out driving harness horses – hackneys, that sort of thing – helping at shows, and playing around stables. Then Frank Speakman started training at Southport and I began to ride a bit of work for him. That was just after the Second World War.'

When he left school, he worked full-time as a stable lad and continued to do so until National Service claimed him. Some fortunate young men were able to profit from their two years' service in the forces and further their civilian careers. Donald McCain was not one of them and when he returned to civilian life he was happy to rejoin the Southport stable. Happy for a time, that is. The trainer was preparing for a move to Cheshire and Donald could see a path up a dead-end, so he broke with racing and bought himself an old taxi. 'And I built up from there.'

The taxi did good business and soon he launched a fleet of private-hire cars. Car sales followed after that as he continued to make a success of his business. And even while he was getting the business off the ground and spending much of his time behind the wheel of a taxi, he maintained his active interest in National Hunt racing. 'I always had a racehorse about the place. Usually I had them given to me – old, broken-down horses. One of them was San Lorenzo.'

San Lorenzo had been one of the best chasers in Neville Crump's Middleham stable in the late '50s and had started favourite, with second top weight, in the National Hunt Handicap Chase at the Cheltenham Festival meeting in 1960. He moved from Neville Crump's stable to that of George Owen the next season, having won nine times, and brought his score to ten at Birmingham, now defunct. Later he broke down and was sent back to Ireland. He was due to be put down when his then owner heard that Donald McCain would be interested in taking him over. He was shipped over from Ireland and trained under permit at Southport.

Thirteen was a lucky age for him; he was enjoying his racing again, and he was only two days into the fourteen-year age group when he won a selling chase at Liverpool which at that time still was staging meetings throughout the season. San Lorenzo was opposed by two twelve-year-olds and a thirteen-year-old and started as the outsider of the four. He fought a stern battle with one of the two youngsters from halfway and pulled himself into a half-length lead on the flat. Only a week went by before San Lorenzo turned out at Haydock.

It was a better seller this time and San Lorenzo was virtually ignored in the betting, yet again he ran a fine race. He held the lead for most of the two miles and compelled the rider of Miserable Monk, an easy winner on his previous outing, to the utmost effort to hold a three-quarter length advantage. Donald McCain's achievement in producing a fourteen-year-old to run two such races within a week after that elderly chaser had been on the racing scrap-heap went unheralded but gave confidence to his young trainer. He also won races with two other moderate old horses and then decided that he should apply for a full licence. 'I had had a permit on or off for a number of years and thought that if I could win races with moderate old animals I might do well with something a bit better. I couldn't afford to get a decent horse of my own and taking out a licence so that I could train for someone else was a way, I hoped, to overcoming that.'

76

He had not had any settled stable premises, using various sites round Southport, and the local sands were his training ground. Some trainers believe that the sands can be very useful as an exercise area when their gallops are too hard, or too wet, and others believe that fast work on sands can adversely affect a horse's action. Very few have even considered working their horses entirely on sand. Donald McCain did so initially because he had no choice. He has continued to do so when he could have taken an alternative and the practise has been vindicated beyond all doubt.

One of his first clients when he started out as a taxi driver was Mr Noel le Mare, a construction engineer from Liverpool. Mr le Mare's childhood was a hard one and he earned his first pennies by selling papers on the street-corners of Liverpool. Now well into his 80s, he remembers the occasion when one of his customers proved to be an American millionaire – and a generous one. He vowed then that he would achieve three things in his life. 'I would make a million myself, marry a beautiful woman and win the Grand National.' By the time that he made acquaintance with Donald McCain his accountant could verify that the first of the three ambitions had been realised and Mr le Mare was in no doubt that the second was a fact of long standing. But the third ambition was proving frustratingly elusive. He reckoned that he himself and his family – by way of presents to him – had spent a small fortune on his quest for a National winner. One especially expensive purchase had not even been sound enough to get on a racecourse at all.

On his journeys with Donald McCain, the trainer recalls, 'we always talked horses'. Both enjoyed the conversations and they were to reap a remarkable harvest for them. It was 1969 when Donald applied for, and was granted, a full licence and at first owners were very hard to come by, as were suitable stable staff. He had a mere half dozen horses in his yard when he set out. One of them was Implicate, a seven-year-old who had won for John Sutcliffe, the Epsom trainer, the previous season and then moved on to Fred Winter. Implicate had not been long at Southport when he ran in the Lodge Handicap Chase at Market Rasen.

Three of the seven runners were at 20 to 1, including Implicate. He won by six lengths, ruining every Tote treble ticket in the process, other winners began to trickle in and the idea began to form in Mr le Mare's mind that he should pursue his search for a Grand National winner through Donald McCain. 'He said, "Get me a horse if you fancy one," and we got Glenkiln for him. Mr le Mare wanted one with the Grand National qualification.'

Glenkiln had been trained by Ken Oliver at Hawick and had begun to disappoint too frequently to be held in the high esteem he had been earlier in his career. He began the 1971–72 season with two disastrous displays, in the second of them hitting almost every fence on the course at Wetherby and finishing tailed off last of four in a two-mile chase. After that he was sent to the Doncaster Sales where lukewarm bidding reached 1,050 guineas. Donald McCain made the last bid and duly reported to Mr le Mare that he had got him a horse to run in the Grand National. 'When I told him how much he was, Mr le Mare said that he couldn't be much good for that sort of money.' He was to have the pleasure of being proved wrong.

Glenkiln had his first race in Mr le Mare's colours at Wetherby on the second day of the Christmas meeting and did far better than on his previous appearance there, finishing third in a two-and-a-half mile chase. Two good displays followed at Haydock and then a minor disaster. Donald, thinking he was declaring Glenkiln to run in the Grand National, in fact declared him as a non-runner.

He felt the disappointment acutely and, characteristically, shouldered the blame for the mistake with total frankness. Mr le Mare was philosophical about the error, cementing even further the happy relationship between the two men; and they compromised by running Glenkiln in the Topham Trophy the Thursday before National day. He jumped well and was with the leaders for more than two miles before weakening into ninth place behind Sunny Lad. Glenkiln had four more races that season and ended with a fifteen-length victory at Cartmel.

'We had one or two useful animals together by then and the job started to click a bit,' Donald explains. Glenkiln was doing well indeed considering his purchase price and his record immediately prior to his sale but there was a doubt about his stamina. Mr le Mare knew that, realistically, he would need to look for another horse if his Liverpool dream were to be realised and he asked Donald McCain to be on the look-out for a likely type. Probably he would not have done so had he been able to foretell the outcome of the William Hill Grand National Trial Chase at Liverpool on October 28 that year.

William Hill's had made a substantial contribution to the prizemoney for the chase and BP had also stepped in to make a return to October racing possible at Liverpool. The Grand National Trial lived up to its title by attracting an excellent field of eleven runners.

The favourite was L'Escargot, winner of the Cheltenham Gold Cup in 1970 and 1971 and one of the best-class horses to run over the Aintree fences since the Second World War. Black Secret, who had dead-heated with General Symons for third place in the Grand National that March behind Well to Do and Gay Trip, was second favourite. Specify, neck winner of the 1971 Grand National over Black Secret, was well fancied, too, as was Sunny Lad, the Topham Trophy winner from Fred Rimell's stable.

Jimmy Bourke, a fine horseman, had the mount on the 16 to 1 Glenkiln and had one of the most memorable rides of his life. The race was over a distance just short of three miles, and over the Grand National fences, As they jumped the Chair, the third fence, Glenkiln held a clear lead he was not to relinquish. Black Secret chased him to the Canal Turn and then back-pedalled and Sunny Lad could not find the pace to trouble him after getting well behind. L'Escargot did move up from the rear to overtake Gyleburn on the flat but made no serious impression on Glenkiln's advantage and was beaten twelve lengths.

The welcome for Glenkiln in the winner's enclosure from Donald McCain and his wife, as from Mr and Mrs le Mare and Glenkiln's lad was in no way inhibited. 'Bloody marvellous,' the trainer told Jimmy Bourke. He was thrilled and he showed it. The racing correspondents got a bagful of quotes which would have taken a week to fill from other sources and Mr le Mare began to reason that the display should make Glenkiln his first choice for the National, whatever Red Rum did in the meantime.

CHAPTER TWELVE

Before Glenkiln won the William Hill Trial he had lost his Liverpool qualification and Donald McCain thought he would have difficulty in regaining it. 'Mr le Mare wanted a Liverpool horse and I thought I had better find him one. Red Rum was qualified and he had run a good race in the Scottish Grand National. He carried bottom weight, I know, but he had made nearly all the running and then had not been beaten far. Obviously he got the trip and the Ayr fences are pretty stiff, so he had the right credentials. And he was the right age.'

Back at Southport, he found Red Rum to be 'a straightforward sort of horse.' Billy Ellison, a married stable-lad, took over the work Sandra Kendall had done with such devotion and it was Red Rum's good fortune that in Billy he found a worthy successor to her. Women as a rule have more patience than men, at least when it comes to tending to the needs of horses, and are far more likely to be tolerant of their whims and fancies. They seek the solution to a problem in kindness and understanding rather than severe rebuke and for that reason are better equipped to persuade a highly-strung thoroughbred to give of his best. But not for Billy Ellison the touch of temper transmitted to the horse through its bit, or the unsympathetic handling dealt out to some horses with Red Rum's liveliness. He sensed the character behind the Red Rum exterior and, without knowing it, stepped accurately into Sandra's shoes.

Donald McCain's description of Red Rum as 'straightforward' is elaborated on : 'He has a lot of vitality, is a very willing

horse, very, very sound, and a great personality.' He reasoned
that as Red Rum was about to begin his sixth season of racing
he should have a routine spiced with plenty of variety. Consequently, he did not confine him to one work rider; occasionally
Billy Ellison handed over to one of the other lads or the head
lad. This has continued to be the case ever since.

Before he went to Doncaster to bid for Red Rum, Donald
asked Tommy Stack about him. Tommy's comments encouraged him and after the sale he asked Tommy if·he would
like to go on riding Red Rum in his races. 'Great; I would love
to,' was Tommy's reply. He had told Donald that Red Rum
jumped well, and stayed, and that he would always win races.
He had also told him that he needed a race or two to get him
really fit.

Donald sketched out a programme for Red Rum, splitting
the season in two. 'The thing was, he was to be our first
National runner and I had never trained a horse to do that sort
of job before. So we were feeling our way with him. He was a
horse who liked the good ground, so we planned to run him
early on. I thought that I could not go on and drag him right
through the middle of the winter and then bring him back fresh,
so I planned to knock it off and bring him back fresh for the
spring. If you have the opportunity of training a horse which
would run well in the National, which I obviously had, you
don't throw the opportunity away.'

His initial assessment of Red Rum took in the view that he
was a horse who needed a lot of work. So after a foundation
had been laid with several weeks of exercise at the slow paces
Red Rum was cantered long and often on Southport sands.
Then came the fast work-outs, in which in the September of
1972 he was accompanied by a bay daughter of the stayer,
Raise You Ten, called Gambling Girl. She had been placed
three times in seven outings over hurdles the previous season.

Now that he had a relatively-expensive horse in his yard,
Donald McCain found persuasive voices trying to turn him
against regular use of the sands. He listened to them, considered
the advice and then rejected it. 'I would be lost without the
sands,' he says. Pat Rohan, whose stables are at Malton, and
Snowy Gray, who trains at Beverley, often take their horses to
East-coast sands in bad springs. They can find long stretches

of safe sand at Filey, or near Bridlington, but they have to make a fairly close study of the tides. At Southport, the tide rarely causes any disturbance of normal routine and if the beach is the epitome of boredom to the mind of a lively young boy it is wonderfully suitable for the training of racehorses.

'The horses can work over stretches of up to a mile and six furlongs, if necessary. You have to go some way out to find sand with the corrugated effect caused by the tide and, anyway, when you harrow it breaks that up.

'We will canter without harrowing but anything over a good, swinging canter is all on a prepared gallop – after the harrow has been along.'

Both Gambling Girl and Red Rum were to have their first races of the new season at Carlisle on September 30th. The month had been an exceptionally dry one and the going at Carlisle was hard. Tommy Stack was engaged to ride both the McCain horses, beginning with Gambling Girl in a division of the Ullswater Novices' Hurdle. The Northern representative of Raceform, that indispensable racing publication, made his customary inspection of the runners in the novice event and marked down 'bit backward' against the name of Gambling Girl. The filly's trainer might not have agreed. Tommy tracked the favourite, Makuti, on her until the last half-mile and sent her on at the third last. The work she had done on the sands paid off and she held her lead to the line.

When trainer and jockey met in the parade ring before the Windermere Handicap Chase – a fairly valuable one for so early in the season, being worth £622 to the winner – Tommy repeated what he had told Donald earlier: 'This fellow won't be ready; he always needs a couple of runs before he is right.' Donald gently suggested that he could be in for a surprise. 'We had been doing quite a bit of graft with him and I replied: "Well, he has been going well with that one who won the first one for you."'

Red Rum was the outsider of the four runners, at 6 to 1. Gyleburn, trained by Gordon Richards and ridden by Ron Barry, had run consistently well earlier in the year though putting Ron Barry on the floor at the first fence in the Grand National won by Well to Do. He was favourite to make a winning reappearance; Proud King, who had won a hurdle race earlier in the month, was second favourite and Nephin Beg, successful a fortnight earlier at Bangor, was at half Red Rum's odds. Gyleburn made the running and by the third from home had shaken off Proud King and Nephin Beg. Red Rum, however, was more persistent in his challenge. The 250-yard run-in is longer than most and it was on it that Red Rum pulled up to Gyleburn and then forged narrowly ahead. Gyleburn could do no more and Red Rum was first home by three-quarters of a length.

'Tommy was surprised, and I was a bit surprised, too,' says the trainer, 'and from then on Red Rum never looked back.' Tommy realised that Donald had indeed been able to give Red Rum a lot of work on the sands. 'He jumped really well that day,' he adds. As if to emphasise how forward the McCain string was, Golden Blue won a selling hurdle on the second day of the Carlisle meeting and Glenkiln finished within six lengths of the useful Red Swan in a two-mile chase the same day. It constituted the trainer's best-ever start to a season.

Tommy's retainer for Tom Jones prevented his riding Red Rum in his next outing, in the Gordon Foster Handicap Chase at Wetherby on October 11. Instead Tommy went to Cheltenham where he repeated an earlier victory on Cannelloni in a division of a novices' hurdle. Ron Barry took over on Red Rum and began the day by winning the seller again on Golden Blue, a horse bought out of a seller very cheaply by Donald McCain. That particular Wetherby seller was not a satisfactory one in some respects, though Golden Blue did his best and was not the subject of criticism.

Red Rum carried a 5 lb. penalty in the Gordon Foster and still was set to receive 22 lb. from the course specialist, Supermaster, and 16 lb. from Esban. Ballysagert, Arthur Stephenson's talented young chaser, patently needed the outing and drifted in the betting from 5 to 1 to double those odds. Red Rum's earlier victory had not greatly impressed the bookmakers and both Supermaster and Esban were preferred to him in the betting. The lead alternated between the three best-fancied horses until approaching the last, plain, fence down the York-road side of the course. There Ron Barry asked Red Rum to step up the pace and within a hundred yards the whole complexion of the race changed. Supermaster, suddenly feeling the strain, weakened quickly under his big weight and Esban, who had been struggling from halfway, fell even further behind. Ballysagert, by virtue of some faultless jumping, moved past both of them but without posing the slightest threat to Ron Barry.

Newcastle, a course which has thrived under the direction of Freddie Newton, staged an exceptionally good programme for a mid-week fixture a fortnight later. It featured the £5,000 Fighting Fifth Hurdle in which Tingle Creek, a versatile American six-year-old, was due to oppose the progressive Comedy of Errors and a brave little Yorkshire hurdler, Easby Abbey, who were to fill first and second places later in the season in the Champion Hurdle. Tingle Creek had joined Tom Jones and so Tommy Stack was able to fulfil his retainer and still ride Red Rum in the Salamanca Handicap Chase, a £1,000 event. It was a race which was to have great significance for Tommy and one which made him look at Red Rum in a new light.

'I really murdered the horse; I was off the bridle with a full circuit to go,' he remembers. The gallop set by Ron Barry on Off the Cuff was strong and though he and the well-backed Tregarron had had enough before the turn for home Ballysagert clearly had not. John Enright had held him back for the first two miles and, brought on by his Wetherby race, he soon jumped his way to the front when encouraged to go forward to the leaders. With two fences to go, Ballysagert was several lengths ahead of Red Rum, on whom Tommy was riding his hardest. If Red Rum had a flaw in his courage then was the time for it to show. Yet the more Tommy demanded of him, the more he gave. And it was Ballysagert not Red Rum who began to flag on the approach to the final fence.

On the flat, Ballysagert's stride shortened. Red Rum's, if anything, lengthened and three strides from the post he caught the leader. 'I had given him a very hard race and I thought it would be a while before he would win again,' Tommy adds. Another surprise was in store for him. Red Rum showed no ill-effects at all, ate with his customary heartiness and was so full of bounce that Donald McCain decided to let him run again at Haydock, just ten days after the Newcastle battle. The race was the appropriately-named Southport Handicap Chase and in it Red Rum had to carry an 8 lb. penalty for his most recent victories. The Inventor, Brian Fletcher's Grand

National mount of the previous season, had won a minor hurdle race by twelve lengths first time out and obviously had trained on. He was made second favourite along with Red Rum's rival of old, Fortune Bay II.

When the two had met at Catterick during Red Rum's last season at Oxclose, Fortune Bay had carried 3 lb. more than Red Rum and had beaten him by five and a half lengths. This time, Red Rum's penalty had taken him 7 lb. above Fortune Bay in the weights. On the basis of a length to a pound, therefore, Fortune Bay should have had a decided advantage but racehorses are less predictable than the the the bookmakers' Rolls-Royces.

'I thought he couldn't possibly come out a fresh horse,' says Tommy. That feeling was reflected to a certain extent in the betting for after opening at 13 to 8, Red Rum went out to 2 to 1. Fortune Bay's jumping was not accurate enough for him to stay in the picture and Indian Yeldah, having his first run of the season, set the early pace. Garpin, a useful handicap chaser, took over after the first mile but Tommy sensed straight away that neither he nor The Inventor, who was galloping alongside, was going to cause him any trouble. Five fences out, Red Rum moved to the front and the result was determined. 'He won on the bridle: I was very impressed with him. He ran a two-stone better horse than at Newcastle,' Tommy adds.

'The change of stables obviously had done him a lot of good; plus, I think, working on the sands. This had altered him a lot. Don McCain had done a marvellous job on the horse. I'll have to give the horse himself some of the credit for the improvement, too,' Tommy states. 'He must have improved with age, and Don McCain is the first to admit this. You get this with a lot of jumpers: they are no good at five, then they get to seven or eight and they are good horses.'

Red Rum was still only seven and was showing a zest for racing which, combined with his accurate, careful jumping and his surprising stamina, was making him into a very complete performer. 'We were just feeling our way with him,' says Donald McCain. He was convinced that there was considerably more improvement in Red Rum and that it would be revealed in due course.

The first part of his campaign for the season was drawing to a close and the time had come, the trainer thought, to resolve all doubts about the Grand National arrangements. When Red Rum came back in the spring he must have a jockey who was going to ride him in all his races, so that when they went to Liverpool both would be fully prepared and with a sound understanding one of the other.

He had thought of giving Red Rum an introduction to the Grand National fences in the William Hill Trial Chase at the October meeting and discussed this with Tommy. 'I said, "No, Don, don't run the horse: we'll take the horse to Liverpool once and that's for the National. He is a clever horse and you don't want to go there too often." He agreed and asked me if I would ride him in the National. I said, "I'd love to but I don't know if I'll be able." ' The Tom Jones retainer would probably claim him for Ashville, the same age as Red Rum and regarded as one of the most promising staying chasers in the country. So a decision about Red Rum's Grand National jockey was postponed for a while, and Glenkiln deputised for Red Rum in the William Hill Chase – with such happy results.

After Red Rum's Haydock triumph, Donald McCain sought clarification from Tommy and was told that he would have to partner Ashville. The trainer replied that, in those circumstances, he would have to get another jockey lined up – 'Somebody good.' His choice fell on Brian Fletcher for it seemed to him that Brian had exactly the credentials needed, and he was not tied to a retainer as, for instance, was Ron Barry who had already won on Red Rum.

'I had ridden a couple of horses for Don McCain one day at Carlisle, at the time that I was on the crest of a wave before my Teesside fall. I didn't know the man from Adam then, and I remember that one of the two fell. Anyway, when he asked me ride Red Rum up at Ayr in mid-November, 1972, I was only too pleased to do so for I had known the horse since he was a two-year-old and I had retained a great admiration for him. Don had run him four times and won four times with him, and obviously the horse was still improving,' says Brian.

He remembers Red Rum's first racecourse appearance, at Liverpool, and the way in which he finished to force a dead-heat. 'He even caught my eye then, when he returned to the unsaddling enclosure, and he did so again in his early days over hurdles.' Brian particularly recalls Red Rum's drawing away to beat his mount, New Brighton, at Wetherby and his victory over At Ease in his following race, at Nottingham. 'As a two-year-old, he was a good-looking stamp of a horse. He had improved by the time he won that Doncaster seller as a three-year-old and now he is a really perfect example of a steeple-chaser. You think when you look at him, "How on earth can he run four and a half miles and come back looking just the same?" He does keep his condition remarkably well.'

Brian knew him in 1972 as a horse who always had possessed plenty of ability. 'Not knowing how he was trained, and so on, I can't say much more but there was a feeling before Don McCain got him that he did not always do his best.'

Red Rum was driven up to Ayr, where he had been a visitor so often in the past, nine days after his Haydock victory in preparation for the Mauchline Handicap Chase on the Monday. The handicapper had reassessed him after his first three wins of the season and the fourth had brought Red Rum a 4 lb. penalty. This meant that Slave's Dream, who had been set to concede 7 lb. to Red Rum in the Scottish Grand National now received 1 lb. from him. Quick Reply, winner of that Scottish National when conceding 2 lb. to Red Rum, also received 1 lb. In fact, both were having their first runs of the season and neither was strongly fancied to beat Red Rum, a very firm favourite at 11 to 8. There was some money for Hurricane Rock, ridden by Ron Barry for his retaining stable. He had been runner-up to Sunny Lad in the Topham Trophy and had proved his ability to stay the distance of three miles and three furlongs.

'He jumped impeccably,' says Brian. 'I hit the front turning for home, and he kept going relentlessly to win quite easily, really.' That performance taught him a lot about the horse. 'You couldn't just go to the front when you thought so; you had to make up your mind in good time because he was a lazy sort. He jumped very well and he stayed, and you had to to make full use of those abilities.' Slave's Dream and Quick Reply could not hold Red Rum in the last mile and though Hurricane Rock plodded on Red Rum had far too much pace for him. The six-length margin could have been extended.

Brian had encouraging words for Red Rum's trainer as he

dismounted. 'Well, Mr McCain, this horse undoubtedly is a good horse, undoubtedly he stays and he jumps; if he runs in the National I would love to ride him. This is a typical National horse.' Not that Red Rum was the horse he became later. 'He did not give me the feeling he was to in later races; he had, after all, had five quick races and Don McCain didn't know as much about him as he did later. And Red Rum was not so developed physically, though still strong and good-looking. He has shown since then that the more you know of him, of his habits and his ways, the better because he is a great character.'

Donald McCain adhered to his plan and gave Red Rum a rest in mid-season. The weather had been unusually kind and the going, which had been good at Ayr, predictably deteriorated. The Haydock and Newcastle meetings in late January were abandoned because of frost and snow, so while other trainers fretted Donald McCain could remain content that at least his programme for Red Rum was not being thrown out of gear.

CHAPTER THIRTEEN

While Red Rum rested in his Southport box and was restricted to gentle exercise, Brian Fletcher continued to ride winners. Tony Dickinson, whose ratio of victories to runners is the best of any trainer in Britain, put him up on Kilmoyler at Catterick in mid-January. He was delighted with the outcome and Brian won further races on him at Sedgefield and Teesside Park. By that time, he had been told by Donald McCain that Red Rum was back in fast work and – weather permitting – would begin the road to Liverpool in the Cumberland Grand National Trial Chase at Carlisle on January 31, exactly two months before Grand National day.

The mild winter weather went on and the ground was good when Brian walked into the parade ring to meet the trainer. He had not seen Red Rum since Ayr and, in fact, not once in his record-breaking association with him was to ride him out at Southport. That part of Red Rum's preparation always was left to Billy Ellison, or to the head lad, or, occasionally, to another of the lads. There were three other horses walking round with Red Rum, and all three were at shorter prices, though only marginally.

Gyleburn, who had been beaten by Red Rum over the same course and distance back in September, had been running well in the meantime. He had been conceding 8 lb. to Red Rum on that occasion; now Red Rum's improvement was acknowledged by the handicapper and they met at level weights.

Bountiful Charles, a remarkable novice trained by Sir Guy

Cunard, was joint favourite with Gyleburn. He had won five times and was to win three more races before the end of the season. It is one of the strangest phenomena of racing that Sir Guy, possibly the best point-to-point jockey of all time, has had very few horses in his stable since he took out a licence after severely injuring his neck in a fall at the Derwent point-to-point. Give him the horse and he will get the results. Making up the Carlisle quartet was Master Val, second to Bountiful Charles in a three-mile novice chase at Newcastle in November. He was a tough, dour stayer.

Ron Barry, well on the way to his first championship, made the running on Gyleburn. Jonjo O'Neill, deputising for Ron Barry who was claimed by his stable for Gyleburn, pushed Bountiful Charles along in second place, just in front of Red Rum. John Enright held up Master Val in last place. The pace was slow and when Ron Barry kicked on approaching the fourth last Master Val found his more experienced opponents too fast for him. Not so, Bountiful Charles. He caught Gyleburn just before the last and, powerfully ridden by young O'Neill, pulled away to win by a length and a half. Red Rum gained ground on both of them towards the finish and at the post only a short head separated him from Gyleburn. Brian was more than pleased with him and Donald McCain delighted that he had come back from his lay-off to do so well in a slowly-run race. He was learning more and more about the horse and his requirements.

Already he had learned that Red Rum thrived on racing and, accordingly, he took him to his local course – Haydock – eight days after Carlisle for the Haydock Park National Trial. Red Rum was placed 5 lb. above Gyleburn in the handicap this time and again Gyleburn was preferred to him in the betting. Well to Do, the National hero of the previous season, had won a race named after him at Towcester in the January, and was joint second favourite with Gyleburn. Southern Lad, who it was thought might have won the Great Yorkshire Chase at Doncaster but for unseating his rider, was the favourite. Red Rum satisfied jockey and trainer by finishing second to Highland Seal, a very useful and versatile stayer and not the indifferent performer his starting price of 25 to 1 might suggest. Red Rum was giving 12 lb. to him and that was no easy task.

It was encouraging that Red Rum had decisively turned the tables on Gyleburn, beaten seven lengths, and that he had been able to drop a good handicap chaser like Proud Tarquin in the last half-mile. Three miles, it seemed, was now a minimum distance for Red Rum: four and a half could be much better for it was towards the end of the third mile that he was putting in his best work. Brian retained the opinion that he was a lazy horse but there was to be no return to blinkers. There were still seven and a half weeks to go to the National and if Red Rum was to go there as a fresh horse his programme would have to be curtailed. Donald McCain checked his calendar and put a mark against the Greenall Whitley Chase, again at Haydock, on March 3.

It rained heavily in the north towards the end of February and on the first day of the Haydock meeting the going was soft on the hurdles course, although officially described as good on the chase course. Brian rode Stag Party for Jumbo Wilkinson, a very capable Middleham trainer, in the Greenall Whitley Hurdle and won by four lengths after having to work hard to catch Past Master. Overnight rain had its effect on the ground and on the Saturday it was soft, too, on the chase course. Donald McCain was as firm in his conviction that Red Rum was not fully effective on soft ground as the horse's previous trainers had been but there weren't many alternative races left if Red Rum was to have the requisite time between the outing he needed and the National.

The Tunku, bought out of Ken Oliver's stable in the October of 1972, also was entered that day, in the curtain-raiser, the Mad Hatters' Novices' Chase. Brian set the good pace essential to him, for he had proved he could stay three miles and this event was over two, and when he still led at the last victory seemed to be his. He hit the top of it, however, and Woodland Poacher's strong late run deprived him of first prize almost on the post. A tough young jumper of great promise, Woodland Poacher was not to survive his next season. An hour later Brian moved on to the course on Red Rum for the Greenall Whitley, worth just £15 short of £5,000 to the winner. Down at Newbury, an ex-Australian horse called Crisp was being led back to his box having won the two-and-a-half mile Geoffrey Gilbey Memorial Chase.

Splint trouble had kept the giant Crisp off the course between October and February when he has run second to Bali-
nese in the Whitbread Trial Chase at Ascot. He had to give
weight to Leap Frog, Royal Relief and The Laird in the
Geoffrey Gilbey and yet he beat them with ease. Whereupon
Fred Winter shelved his plan to let him have a second crack
at the Cheltenham Gold Cup. The Two-Mile Champion Chase
at Cheltenham became his next objective, with the Grand
National to follow. 'If Crisp can stay the four miles 865 yards
of the Grand National course at Aintree then this season's
National is his for the taking,' wrote Audax's perceptive deputy
in *Horse and Hound*, after witnessing Crisp's annihilation of
top-class handicappers at Ascot.

Red Rum received no such praise after the Greenall Whitley.
With 11 st. 2 lb. to carry, he had only Jomon of the eleven
runners above him in the weights. The early betting skirmishes
saw Red Rum at 9 to 2 and Jomon at 5 to 1. Both weakened,
but Red Rum only by half a point so that he started a clear
favourite at 5 to 1. Six of his protagonists had won on their
previous outings and, overall, the field was of the high quality
expected for so valuable a race – even the fourth horse home
would earn £332.

The testing conditions admirably suited Straight Vulgan, a
seven-year-old trained at that time by J. A. Edwards and
ridden by John Haine. He jumped off in the lead, was passed
by Money Market, and then led again when Money Market
came down towards the end of the second mile. Tregarron, only
six, was sent ahead shortly afterwards at which stage Red
Sweeney and Red Rum had moved into the leading group.

Straight Vulgan, a winner over three miles in deep ground,
Red Sweeney, an out-and-out stayer, and Red Rum were a
powerful trio for a youngster like Tregarron to have to hold
off but, with the assistance of his courageous and gifted young
rider, Colin Tinkler, he did so with a wide margin of safety.
Straight Vulgan took second place, seven lengths behind him
and half a length in front of Red Sweeney, who kept Red Rum
out of third place by the same distance. Tregarron, who was
completing a hat-trick in handicaps, had not been entered for
the Grand National because of his tender age; his turn was
expected to come the next season yet he was not to fulfil the

promise of his six-year-old days after being a victim of the cough.

Red Rum's performance was not one of his best, it had to be admitted, but he had made one fairly serious error and with Tregarron out of the way it would have been a close thing. And, of course, there had been the soft ground. Donald McCain was in no way discouraged. He does not bet, but Mr le Mare had not missed having a bet in the Grand National since he successfully wagered on Eremon in 1907 and he and other owners who had horses with Donald were not dissuaded from taking the (to the trainer) attractive odds on offer about Red Rum for Liverpool. Red Rum would carry several hefty wagers from that source at 33 to 1 and 25 to 1. Now all that remained was for Donald McCain to make sure that he gave Red Rum all the work he needed in the four full weeks left to him.

'You have this query all the time, "Are you doing the right thing?" I was playing it by ear and, to be honest, I was very severe on him between Haydock and the National,' says Donald McCain. 'He did a tremendous amount of work.'

Meanwhile, the bookmakers were having apparent difficulty in finding an ante-post favourite. Maybe Cheltenham would clear the air. There, on the first day, Crisp was to tackle the Irish-trained, American-bred Inkslinger and Royal Relief, the title-holder, in the National Hunt Two-Mile Champion Chase. He would start at odds on and if he ran up to expectations he would become a positive National fancy, even if Cheltenham could not tell anything relevant about his suspect stamina. So to a lovely Tuesday at a glorious course where the view from the stands is breath-taking. Having conceded 9 lb. to Royal Relief at Ascot and beaten him by eleven lengths Crisp could hardly fail to beat him at level weights, said reason, so Crisp was at 15 to 8 on and Royal Relief at 14 to 1 against.

There was not one moment in the race when Crisp was racing with the authority he had been expected to, and Inkslinger and Royal Relief led him as they swept down the hill to the final turn. Even up the hill, Crisp could not make any impression on them and the subdued Englishmen had to let the Irish cheers ring round them as Inkslinger fought on to a brave victory.

'Two miles is too short for him now,' said Fred Winter,

Crisp's trainer, after Richard Pitman had dismounted. He did not accept the evidence of the 1972 Gold Cup which suggested that Crisp did not stay more than three miles. Crisp had been favourite for that race as well and had faded abruptly in that last taxing three furlongs as Glencaraig Lady, perhaps luckily, held off Royal Toss and The Dikler. After the first three there had been a seven-length gap to L'Escargot and Crisp. But Fred Winter thought that the Crisp of 1973 was to some extent a changed horse. Racing over longer distances than two miles had taken the edge off his speed and had helped to develop stamina, and he had, after all, beaten The Dikler over three miles in the previous season. Top weight of 12 st. was a daunting burden but at 17 hands 1 in. in height he had the build for the job and his brilliant jumping just might enable him to last home.

Another leading Grand National fancy was not to have an outing before Liverpool. She was Princess Camilla, the mount of Ron Barry. After a good win at Nottingham, Princess Camilla had been ridden with a trifle too much enterprise at Wetherby and a twenty-length lead had evaporated in the final quarter of a mile in the Rowland Meyrick Chase. She had returned to outstay Rouge Autumn and Esban in the four-mile Warwick National. She could jump and she would have a superb horseman on her back.

After a poor run behind Bountiful Charles at Wetherby in late February, Ashville came back into the reckoning with a much-improved performance in the National Hunt Handicap Chase at Cheltenham. Tommy Stack, out of action through injury, had Jeff King as his deputy and Ashville raised considerable hopes for Liverpool by finishing second to Tony Dickinson's The Chisler. Straight Vulgan was three lengths behind him in third place and in that performance lay encouragement for the connections of Red Rum who in a strict interpretation of the Haydock form was 15 lb. better than Straight Vulgan

On the last day of the Cheltenham Festival meeting, L'Escargot made his fourth appearance in the Cheltenham Gold Cup. His form since finishing fourth in the 1972 event had fluctuated from very good – he had beaten Spanish Steps in the Sundew Chase at Haydock and had been second to the smart Sea Brief at Punchestown – to bad, seventh of eight to finish to Sea Brief in the Leopardstown Chase. He had experienced training diffi-

culties before the Leopardstown Chase and with that performance uppermost in the minds of punters started at 20 to 1 for
the Gold Cup. He ran well, being there with a chance at the
third last and eventually taking fourth place, eleven lengths
behind The Dikler.

Spanish Steps was seven lengths in arrears and as he had to
give only 1 lb. to Spanish Steps at Liverpool, where he had
joint top weight with Crisp, Irish confidence grew that he
might make up for his ill-luck in the 1972 National, when
knocked over early in the race. The only other national acceptor
to figure prominently in the betting was Canharis, the Neville
Crump former point-to-pointer.

Both Ladbrokes and William Hill's had been happy to quote
him at 33 to 1 after an exceptionally game win over The Chisler
at Doncaster in late February but The Chisler's subsequent win
at Cheltenham had enhanced the value of that form and his
National odds had contracted accordingly. Canharis's background was the same as that of Sheila's Cottage, Teal and
Merryman II, Neville Crump's previous National winners. He
was not as robust as them, however, and his trainer had dis-
covered that he ran best when absolutely fresh. He planned
to give Canharis little work before Liverpool in sharp contrast
to the plans for Red Rum.

Donald McCain's objective all along was to vary Red Rum's
routine so that however much he was asked to do he continued
to enjoy his work. He achieved his aim and when the Friday
before Grand National Saturday arrived Red Rum was bursting
with health and enthusiasm. Along with Glenkiln, he was
walked from the stables behind the McCain garage premises
down to the sands for his final work-out. Seven furlongs at a
good gallop was the intended exercise, and Donald positioned
himself at the end of the seventh furlong. With him was a
friend who had some useful horses in training and was accus-
tomed to seeing them exercised.

He showed a keen interest as Red Rum and Glenkiln strode
out towards them, their riders not holding back anything in
reserve. His reaction when the trainer sent the two horses back
for another go brought a smile to the trainer's face. 'I wasn't
quite happy with them and after I had told the lads to repeat
the gallop this friend look cross-eyed at me. He didn't say any-

95

thing then but he told me afterwards that he thought they had been asked to do a little bit too much,' Donald recalls.

'I don't think they had. Both horses came back and got stuck into their mangers. They had enjoyed the work; relished it.'

Liverpool is a mere fifteen miles form Donald McCain's yard, a fact which has had some influence on his not looking too hard for alternative premises in a spot more accessible for the majority of racecourses. At that time, his yard was more than adequate. When Red Rum was in the middle of his early-season campaign there were just ten boxes in the yard, eight of which were occupied.

Being so close to Liverpool meant that Red Rum and Glen-kiln could be driven over in mid-morning. The day began for Billy Ellison before six o'clock. He looked in to Red Rum's box, thankfully noted that all was well with him, and then led him out for ten minutes. After that Red Rum had his feed. That left plenty of time in which to strap him out and plait him up before leaving him for an hour or more of total quiet. At ten o'clock the box was driven into the yard and the two horses began the journey to the last Grand National meeting staged by Mrs Mirabel Topham.

Brian Fletcher had missed the first two days of the meeting in order to ride at Teesside Park. He signalled his good form with a hard-earned victory on Royal Gown in a novices' hurdle, forcing him into the lead in the closing stages as Chase Me, a former David Robinson horse, failed to quicken. In fact, Chase Me had broken down. Two seasons later he was still on the injured list and had one abortive visit to the Doncaster sales behind him. Chase Me's owner had paid 4,000 guineas for him at the Newmarket Autumn Sales in 1972. His fortune contrasted sharply with that of Mr Noel le Mare.

After Teeside, Brian drove down to Liverpool where he was to partner Irish Special in the B.P. Shield Handicap Hurdle, an hour and a quarter before the National.

Irish Special came within three-quarters of a length of taking third place in a field of twenty. Then it was time for Brian to join the other thirty-seven jockeys with rides in the Grand National. As he changed into the colours of Mr Le Mare – maroon, with a large yellow diamond on the body – the public poured their money on to his mount. Initially, he was at 12 to

1, two points shorter than Crisp and L'Escargot. Before long he was down to 9 to 1, at which price he was joined by Crisp. Several of the leading racing correspondents had decided in favour of Crisp, basing their belief that he would last out the four and a half miles on his possession of 'class'. In other words, he was superior in ability to the other runners to such an extent that this would offset any deficiency in stamina, this despite his burden of 12 st. Class is, indeed, tangible. The handicapper says so every time he deals with a race. To him, Crisp and L'Escargot had class, and so, too, had Spanish Steps.

For years, there had been a tendency to decry the National as a marathon for moderate handicappers. Well, those critics had their answer in 1973. The top three in the handicap were all first-class horses over park courses and there was some reasonable talent down below, including Proud Tarquin – 'My best ride since Carrickbeg,' said Lord Oaksey – the front-running Grey Sombrero, victor in the Whitbread Gold Cup, and, on 10 st. 5 lb., Red Rum. Peter Scott, that most reliable of racing correspondents, made him the nap selection in the *Daily Telegraph*. Most others at least included him in their likely half-dozen.

Brian Fletcher found the tension building up inside him on the morning of the race and he knew it would stay with him until the starter sent the runners on their way. 'It is not nerves; not the feeling of apprehension which can affect your riding. More is it the consciousness that this is what the events of the racing year have been leading up to. The other races have come and gone; this is the big one. And if you are on a well-backed horse this adds to the tension.

'The trainer, of course, has his share of tension too. He has had the responsibility of preparing the horse for the most important day in his career. But when it comes down to it, the jockey is the man with the ultimate responsibility. The weight in the end is on his shoulders. One mistake and a year's work can be ruined.'

He met Donald McCain and his attractive wife in the parade ring, along with Mr and Mrs Le Mare. The eyes of all four were also on Glenkiln. Remembering Glenkiln's magnificent victory in the William Hill Trial, Mr le Mare had just as much regard for the chance of Glenkiln as he had for that of Red

Rum, possibly more. Jonjo O'Neill, one of the best young riders to emerge in the post-war years, was on Glenkiln. He was a fair prospect but Donald McCain, unlike his owner, had a decided preference for the chance of Red Rum. He looked a picture in the parade ring, strong, well muscled-up, good-looking and well-balanced. If he could realise all the dreams which went out with him, he would not look out of place in the winner's enclosure for sure.

CHAPTER FOURTEEN

An indication of how firm the ground was had come on the Thursday in the Topham Trophy. Inch Arran, in the Queen Mother's colours, had won in a time 10·60 seconds below average. It was faster ground still that Saturday, March 31, and if Donald McCain had been able to choose its condition he would not have made any amendments. He felt sure that Red Rum would get the good gallop that he needed to bring all his stamina into play. How right he was!

Red Rum behaved impeccably throughout the parade in front of the stands. Brian Fletcher was able to disguise the impatience he himself felt, but Ron Barry had an anxious time on Princess Camilla. She broke out into a sweat and became so much on edge that Walter Wharton, her trainer, went out to hold her and try to calm her down. Ron was putting up 4 lb. overweight on her, the same amount as Jeff King put up on Ashville; David Mould added 5 lb. to the burden of Petruchio's Son and David Nicholson 5 lb. to that of Highland Seal. The American amateur, George Sloan, and the gallant 54-year-old Duke of Alburqueque were just 3 lb. above their stipulated weights on Fortune Bay II – now with Josh Gifford – and Nereo respectively.

Brian Fletcher, virtually as light as he had been when weighing out to ride Red Alligator, had not found it necessary to visit the Turkish Baths, and that was just as well. He was about to have one of the most exhausting rides of his life, though elation would mask the tiredness. Richard Pitman was hopeful that Crisp was about to make up for the harsh disappointments of Cheltenham, where Pendil had the Cheltenham

Gold Cup snatched from his grasp after being taken to the front too soon. He had gallantly accepted the blame for that defeat, though as Ivor Herbert reveals in his delightfully evocative 'Winter's Tale' he had been riding to orders.

In their thorough way, Fred Winter and Richard Pitman had walked the course and had formulated their plans for Crisp. 'I was supposed to be fifth or sixth, very, very handy,' Richard said later. Donald McCain did not tie his jockey to any orders because he knew that Brian, though a month short of his twenty-sixth birthday, had great experience of the Aintree course. Brian intended to adhere to the policy which had succeeded so well on Red Alligator. 'I wanted to ride a waiting sort of a race.' He was not alone in that.

Lord Leverhulme, the Senior Steward, had the task of delivering the traditional advice to the jockeys before they went out to ride in the National. The advice was particularly pertinent because of the fast ground. 'Don't go too fast too soon.' A lack of regard for such a warning had led to disaster in the past. The warning was heeded and as the thirty-eight runners swept towards the first fence the pace was sensible. Only Richeleau failed to survive it, inflicting a broken collar bone on Neil Kernick. Remarkably, he was the only rider to suffer anything worse than mild concussion.

Black Secret just led at the first, from Grey Sombrero, Endless Folly, Ashville and Crisp. Red Rum, towards the outside, was a few lengths further back. He jumped it perfectly, as he did the next. Crisp was not only faultless, he attacked the fences with an elan and efficiency which was breath-taking to watch and awe-inspiring for his jockey. Grey Sombrero was no slow-coach in the air but even he was outjumped by Crisp at the second. Here, Richard Pitman scrapped his pre-race plan.

'It is silly to give ground away that you have gained in the air,' he explained later. So rather than restrain Crisp he sat against him and let him go on in the lead. By contrast, L'Escargot was jumping hesitantly in the second half of the field and Princess Camilla was climbing over the fences rather than jumping them. Becher's Brook, the sixth fence, found Crisp with a definite advantage over Grey Sombrero. Black Secret, Rouge Autumn, Hurricane Rock, Endless Folly, Sunny Lad and Great Noise were in the chasing group and behind them came a whole line of horses among whom were Red Rum and Proud Tarquin, their riders quite content and sensing that the pace was much too hot to last.

Everything was going according to plan for Red Rum. Brian had moved him up to thirteenth position as they went sharply left at the first Canal Turn and began to work his way forward. But Crisp had jumped and galloped his way into a gigantic lead by Grand National standards and was going ominously well for those close enough behind to appreciate that it was him and not an outsider being ridden into the ground for five minutes of glory. 'It was a good two-mile chase speed; they went that damned fast,' says Brian.

To one onlooker at least, it seemed that Crisp erred slightly at the Chair. Richard Pitman was unconcerned. 'He just caught his hindlegs in it, but he had stood off and he jumped it superbly. I think he pitched slightly on landing, but no bother.' Away went Crisp on the second circuit after taking the water while the nearest of his pursuers was only at the Chair.

Grey Sombrero headed those pursuers but he broke his shoulder on landing. It seemed a mild mistake and nowhere near bad enough to cause so serious an injury. As he lay injured, the 100 to 1 Endless Folly took over second place. Brian regards the Chair as potentially the most dangerous fence of all, being so narrow in width and so high, and he steered a careful course to it, on the outside of Sunny Lad, Rouge Autumn and Great Noise, who pecked on landing. Great Noise's mistake enabled Red Rum to move into fifth place at the water. Brian could see Crisp striding on to the seventeenth fence.

'Realising this horse was so far in front, realising it was Crisp and knowing the class of the horse, I knew I could not afford to hang about. I knew that he would not come back. Crisp was jumping fantastically well.'

As he landed over the open ditch, the third fence on the circuit and the nineteenth in all, he made up his mind to go in pursuit of Crisp. 'From that point onwards I was never looking over my shoulder wondering what was happening. All I was concentrating on was trying to catch Crisp.' Twenty-five horses had still been standing as they left the grandstands for the last time but Red Rum was the only one able to muster the pace and the energy to go after the brilliantly-agile leader.

'He hurdled Becher's the second time, giving me the most fantastic jump I have had in my life,' said Richard. That leap left him some forty lengths ahead of the chasing Red Rum Next came Spanish Steps, Rouge Autumn, Black Secret and Hurricane Rock. Lord Oaksey had the frustrating experience of being on a horse – Proud Tarquin – who was going strongly enough but on the firm ground simply could not go fast enough. Much further behind, L'Escargot was beginning to lose his hesitancy and to work his way through the stragglers.

At Valentine' Brook, the twenty fifth of the thirty fences, Brian became even more anxious. 'Crisp was so far in front and still he didn't seem to be coming back.' He had no thought other than to continue the chase. 'If I had for a moment said to myself that I wouldn't catch him and had thought of settling for second place that would have been that. Instead I said to myself, "This horse stays well, he jumps well and I want to win the National." '

All was still well for Richard Pitman. Crisp's lead did not diminish noticeably on the run to the plain five-foot fence after Valentine's or on the approach to last of the ditches before the Melling Road. 'I would be at least thirty lengths behind there,' says Brian. Still there was no encouragement to be gleaned from the horse and jockey in front. And then, at long last, came the glimmer of hope he had been waiting for. 'When jumping the second last I saw Crisp's old tail move once or twice. I knew then that I was in with a chance if I could keep going.' What the racegoers at Aintree that day saw perhaps in more accurate detail than the millions of television viewers was the most thrilling and moving climax to a Grand National in modern times.

Richard Pitman, as eloquent as he is capable, takes up the story. 'I was riding what was basically a non-stayer. Therefore, I had to keep hold of his head for as long as I could. The moment a non-stayer comes off the bridle and you start pushing you are in trouble. When you have an out-and-out stayer you can push for ever and they keep finding a bit more.'

'I could feel the signs of tiredness well before the last. I sat a little quiet going into the last, desperately trying to keep him balanced and in a straight line, to pop it and set sail for the winning post.' Up in the stands Fred Winter fully appreciated the situation and, keeping his glasses trained on Crisp, said to his owner 'Start praying, Sir Chester, for you're going to be beat.'

Richard Pitman had taken a look behind at the Canal Turn – 'I was a long way in front but it is a long way from home.' And he had another quick look round as he went to the last. Then he saw Red Rum still some twenty lengths behind. 'But Crisp tripped over it, and wandered, and rolled, and even went violently left-handed half way up the run-in because he was bewildered, he was tired. The jam stick (as we call it) wasn't coming any nearer; it was getting further and further away with every stride.'

Brian also took preventative measures against any wavering on the part of Red Rum. 'After going more than four miles, a horse tends to run off a true course. I was catching Crisp but I knew that if my horse had gone off a true line I would never get to him. As I was approaching Crisp, if Red Rum had ducked in behind him that would have been my race lost. So I had to pull the stick through a couple of times to my left to keep him straight.'

If the shortest route from the last fence to the winning post had been marked in white paint Red Rum's route could hardly have been improved upon. Crisp, after swerving and wobbling to the left as exhaustion drained his legs of strength, lost his action but straightened after the elbow round the Chair fence, where the running rail begins. 'The rail helped him just to plod on. Without the rail from the elbow I'd have been beaten much further than I was,' says Richard Pitman.

With the crowd torn between a desire for Crisp to hold on as a reward for his unsurpassed brilliance over the fences, and his truly wonderful feat in making his burden of 12 st. seem a low not a high weight, and admiration for Red Rum's tenacity in chasing so hard and for so long, the ideal result would have been a dead-heat. If the distance of the race had been four miles and 846 yards the judge might well have decided thus. But there were ten more yards to cover and in those ten yards Red Rum, still galloping whereas poor Crisp's pace had slowed almost to a walk, first caught Crisp and then pulled three-quarters of a length in front.

'My horse gave his all, but gave out just before the line,' said Richard Pitman, whose disappointment contained not one drop of bitterness. 'All I could think of was, "Hurray for such a game horse," ' said Brian Fletcher of his second Grand National winner.

It had been a two-horse race and Golden Miller's thirty-eight-year-old record time had been smashed by almost nineteen seconds. L'Escargot's time would have been good enough to win in most years, even when the ground was so firm. The Irish horse had made up an enormous amount of ground from the second Canal Turn to finish twenty-five lengths behind Crisp. There was a twelve-length gap then to Spanish Steps and then came Rouge Autumn, Hurricane Rock and Proud Tarquin.

The tall figure of Donald McCain could be picked out in the winner's enclosure, his face glowing with pleasure. Mr le Mare and his wife managed to squeeze through the crowd to welcome back their hero, too, and Billy Ellison wept tears of joy for his brave friend. A few feet away, in the adjoining enclosure, stood Fred Winter with Crisp, defeated in the end but a hero beyond all doubt and one with whom Red Rum, one felt, gladly would have shared the limelight.

It has long been the practice at Aintree for the winning jockey, trainer and owner to visit the Press room after the National and give their stories in full to reporters from throughout the world. This time the jockey of the runner-up was invited to join in and, like the admirable sportsman he is, Richard Pitman accepted the invitation. 'If I had made all the running as Richard did and then been beaten when so near to victory I would have locked myself in a cupboard; I couldn't have faced up to people. All credit to Richard for being so good a loser and for giving his story,' says Brian.

Brian took the questioning first. 'Crossing the Melling Road I must have been at least thirty lengths behind . . . The gap was still twenty lengths at the second last . . . I didn't realise that I would win until fifty yards from the post when I saw Crisp falter badly . . . I had to keep hard at my fellow from a long way out to be in with any chance at all . . . he jumped wonderfully well all the way, if he hadn't he would not have won . . . Red Alligator and Red Rum – both very tough horses . . . If I hadn't won I would have lodged an objection on the grounds that the post was too far from the last.'

Mr le Mare, the third of his life's ambitions realised, took over. 'How do I feel? As though I've got some sparrows in my stomach . . . They say I have spent £100,000 in trying to win a National and I wish they wouldn't keep saying that . . . They also say I'm a millionaire; I'd be a bloody fool to be a millionaire at eighty-five years of age . . . William Hill's have just rung me and said they are very sorry Red Rum has won . . . If you had been here for the Grand National Trial and seen Glenkiln you would have had to fancy him too.' Glenkiln had been in the leading dozen and going well when falling at the Chair.

Donald McCain modestly kept in the background Richard Pitman was escorted into the room. 'I want to shake your hand,' he said to Mr le Mare. 'Super.' Mr le Mare replied, 'hard luck.' Obviously he meant it. The Pitman resilience and sportsmanship came out again. 'I suddenly thought half way up the run-in that you had been trying to win a Grand National for fifty years so I took a pull.' The reporters roared with laughter and marvelled at the man. 'If you weren't so handsome I'd kiss you,' answered Mr le Mare, deeply touched by the jockey's warm good humour.

More questions for Richard: 'Did I feel him give out very near to the line? No, no, before the elbow he's gone violently left-handed . . . No jumping mistakes at all, the most fantastic Aintree jumper there has ever been . . . You never have it in your pocket here and I was riding a non-stayer . . . Age? thirty . . . Second before on Steel Bridge; I've got seconditis . . . It's the loneliest feeling in the world when you are out in front on a tiring horse . . . From the last I'm in desperate trouble and I'm going to either just hold out or just get beat and I got beat.'

The Press knew little of Donald McCain. Did he do the fast work on the sands? How long had he had Red Rum? When did he take out a licence? And what about next year? The last question was answered in the same unequivocal way as the remainder. 'Next year, I hope. He will be a much better horse then. We have just been feeling our way with him.' There would be no more races for Red Rum that season. 'He has a nasty overeach low down on on a tendon.'

It was a Press conference epitomising all that is best in National Hunt racing: brave and brilliant horses had been ridden by brave men whose merit went far beyond their ability as jockeys. All those concerned with the equine heroes put those heroes first. Genuine modesty is an endearing quality.

Apart from the Press, there was television to satisfy and radio. Richard Pitman was interviewed by Peter Bromley for B.B.C. Radio and it was suggested that the finish must have been disastrous for him.

He corrected Bromley. 'Hardly disastrous. We are all healthy, the horse is in great fettle and we are just £25,000 worse off than we might have been.' 'But we were weeping tears for you up here and you have bounced back and are actually smiling,' Bromley added in apparent amazement. 'The horse ran a great race; he jumped so fantastically. I will remember that to the end of my days,' Richard explained. 'Great for Brian. He has won it twice, a wonderful feat. He must have worked like the devil to get to me. I was in the enviable position of being in front but he has got the spurs, he was in front on the line and it is great for him, it really is.'

Brian was overjoyed to have won the National for a second time and thoughts of how much he was to receive for having done so were far from his mind. The story had circulated that Mr le Mare was going to reward him with £6,000. It was erroneous. 'I got my ten per cent,' says Brian. 'But I would have done it for sixpence never mind the supposed £6,000.'

Red Rum would have gone for the Scottish Grand National but for his bad overreach. Instead, Donald McCain eased him off. 'He came back very full of himself but I couldn't train him because of the overreach. We waited for the weather and then turned him away. He would be out to grass four weeks after the National, starting with being turned away during the day and brought in at night. Finally, he was turned away completely. No sooner was he out to grass than he had dropped his belly and you would have thought he was an old hunter, not the quality chaser he is. He was entirely different to what he is in training; he is a bright horse, full of enthuiasm, boisterous. Out to grass, he is always the first to come to you. He really enjoys himself.'

He would have a full two months at grass before being brought back to his box and prepared for another season of racing and another Grand National. Donald McCain predicted after the 1973 National that Red Rum could improve by another 20 lb (one pound equals one length). If his prediction proved accurate, Red Rum could keep a step ahead of the handicapper.

CHAPTER FIFTEEN

The programme mapped out for Red Rum in his second season with Donald McCain was to closely resemble that in his first. The September meeting at Perth, however, was a week later and so that was designated for his first outing instead of Carlisle the following week. Donald worked him hard as usual and thought he would pop him over a line of hurdles as a training ingredient. 'He jumped three flights and then said, "Beggar you," and wouldn't do any more.' He did not see this as a reason to enforce discipline. Red Rum did his jumping where it was really necessary, on the racecourse. If he chose not to leave the ground at home, then the old fellow should have his way.

Ignoring the fact that Red Rum had been fit enough to win his first race the previous season, the bookmakers took a chance with him and introduced him into the betting for the Perthshire Challenge Cup at around 4 to 1. The odds-on favourite was Proud Stone, on whom Nick Richards, son of the Penrith trainer, had won an amateur riders' handicap with 12 st. 1 lb. at Worcester a week beforehand. Ron Barry had the ride this time.

Red Rum, carrying 12 st. 4 lb. and conceding 13 lb. to Proud Stone, joined Proud Stone in the lead at the third last, jumped the last alongside him and drew away on the flat to win by a length and a half. In doing so, he went slightly across Proud Stone and though probably the winner on merit lost the race in the stewards' room. That was on Wednesday, September 26. The next Saturday, he went to Carlisle after all for the Windermere Handicap Chase, in which he had beaten Gyleburn on his first outing for Donald McCain.

Once more he had top weight of 12 st. 4 lb., more than a stone above Canharis and 32 lb. more than David French, the horse who had put him on the ground at Catterick. Brian did not hurry him in the first two of the three miles and did not need to thereafter. The leader, Meridian II, unseated his amateur rider at the twelfth and Red Rum was out in front from then on. The official distance was fifteen lengths over James Jacques, the mount of Ron Barry. Canharis was another fifteen lengths back in third place. The time was moderate on the firm ground but Red Rum had done all that Brian had asked him to and Brian was pleasantly surprised that the horse was proving him wrong. His experience with Red Alligator and other National horses had been that they were never the same after Aintree. Red Rum conformed to this impression in that he was not the same – he was better than ever.

On to Ayr next to take on his Haydock conqueror, Tregarron; the very useful stayer Straight Vulgan, now with Gordon Richards; and Tartan Ace, a six-year-old who had joined Arthur Stephenson's stable from Ireland and for whom a bright future was forecast. Compared with the weights they had carried in the Greenall Whitley in the previous March, Tregarron was only 1 lb. worse off though he had beaten Red Rum by eight lengths, and Straight Vulgan was 10 lb. better off though he had been a length in front of Red Rum. Donald McCain's prediction was to undergo a severe test.

The pace was a cracker from the start. Treble Kay made it to the fourteenth and then gave way to Straight Vulgan. Red Rum headed him at the third last only to sacrifice his lead by hitting the last fence low and very hard. Brian sat tight, balanced him and quickly got him going again to win by a length and clip 7·20 seconds of the record for the Ayr three miles and one hundred and ten yards. There were still almost six months to go to the Grand National and one thing was certain, Red Rum would not be near the foot of the handicap this time. He was, indeed, a greatly-improved horse, as he confirmed just over a fortnight later in the John Eustace Smith Trophy Chase at Newcastle where again the going was firm.

Ballysagert, regarded by the handicapper as 18 lb. superior to him a year beforehand, received 4 lb. San-Feliu, a runaway winner at Carlisle, was expected to develop into a fancy for the

National for Neville Crump and though penalised for his win still was a stone and a half below Red Rum. Brian rode Red Rum in the same way he had done in all his races that season, staying in touch with the leaders, moving to the front at the third last and then defying the others to catch him. Again, Red Rum hit the last fence low and again he survived a mistake which would have put down many other chasers. The mistake lost him some ground but not enough to allow San-Feliu to get in a blow.

Meanwhile, another horse had been disproving the theory that they don't come back after a gruelling race in the National. Crisp began his new campaign with a hurdle outing at Worcester in mid-October and, though backward, finished third in a good-class field. After that he went to New-bury for the Hermitage Chase in which first he disposed of Charlie Potheen and Royal Relief and then sustained the gallop so well for the full two and a half miles that the late run of Clever Scot offered no threat at all. Crisp was one of two final acceptors for the Doncaster Pattern Chase on November 10, worth £1,763 to the winner and £422 to the runner-up. The other was Red Rum and they were to meet at level weights, for this time the handicapper had not been called in to do his work.

Donald McCain would not have taken on Crisp had he thought that Red Rum was in for a drubbing, though to most other people it seemed inconceivable that Red Rum could have made the necessary progress to trouble Crisp. After all, he had carried 23 lb. more than Red Rum in the Grand National and at three miles two furlongs, the distance of the Doncaster race, he would have won by some thirty lengths. In the event, Donald was disappointed and most people were proved partly wrong. Red Rum held Crisp to the final straight. He was unable to prevent Crisp drawing into an eight-length lead after that but it was a fine performance, nevertheless, to prevent that eight lengths from growing. It was not unreasonable to suppose that an extra mile and a quarter would have seen Red Rum biting chunks off that lead.

Fine performance or not, Brian Fletcher is convinced that it was not the real Red Rum. 'I don't want to make any excuses for Red Rum; Crisp was a great horse and he may even come out and win the 1975 Grand National. But that was the only time I have ridden Red Rum that he did not give me the right feeling. It's like talking to your wife : one moment she is happy and active and then you may sense that she is down in the dumps. It was like that with Red Rum that day. He did not appear to be enjoying life at all. Maybe because there were only two horses in the race and he felt there was no excitement – I don't know – but he ran like a dead horse.'

Perhaps, therefore, Donald McCain was underestimating the worth of Red Rum's performance when he said at Teeside Park the following Monday that his horse was not quite so improved as he had thought him to be. And perhaps a less modest trainer would have pointed to the fact that on the formbook, Red Rum was 15 lb. better than the previous March and probably, as the distance was too short for Red Rum, decidedly more.

'Maybe I will keep him to Northern handicaps,' he added. It wasn't long, however, before he decided that Red Rum's entry for the Hennessy Cognac Gold Cup at Newbury should stand. Charlie Potheen had to give him a stone and he doubted very much if Fulke Walwyn's horse was equal to that. There were many others who did not and on the day, November 24, Charlie Potheen started favourite in a field of eleven runners.

There was to be no last-fence blunder from Red Rum on this occasion. Sent past Charlie Potheen by Brian at the eighteenth fence, Red Rum lost the lead to Red Candle two out, put in one of the best jumps of his life at the last and got his head in front on the run-in. 'Everything went according to plan. He battled on but Red Candle came again and pipped him on the post, because of the weight,' says Brian. Red Candle, winner in 1972 of the Mackeson Gold Cup, was receiving a stone from Red Rum. That was the sixth outing of the season for Red Rum, all within the space of two months, and Donald McCain thought it enough for the time being.

The programme mapped out by him allowed for an absence from the racecourse of some ten weeks, and the Haydock meeting in the first week of February was to see Red Rum's reappearance. Well, it rained and rained and both days of the Haydock meeting had to be abandoned. So, too, had Carlisle five days later. Still the rain did not relent and still the McCain patience stood the strain. Were the abandonments a blow to him? 'A disappointment more than a blow. You set a programme out and if can follow it things are so much better but if we can get two runs in before the National – he's in at Catterick and Newcastle – we'll be all right,' he said at the time.

The Catterick course is on gravel and is the best-draining course in the North. Had it not been, there would have been no possibility of racing, taking place there on February 20. The surrounding countryside was waterlogged. Racing did go ahead and Brian Fletcher rode the second winner, Scottish Folly, in a two-miles handicap chase. Donald McCain delayed a decision on whether or not to run Red Rum in the Brettanby Handicap Chase until after Scottish Folly's race so that he could have Brian's first-hand information.

It was raining heavily and Brian reported that the ground was bottomless. His words to the trainer were; 'Please, Don, don't run Red Rum. He's a top-of-the-ground horse.' Donald McCain's first reaction was to act on that advice and he went to his travelling head lad to tell him the news. 'Red Rum was so full of himself that he would have ended up hurting himself or somebody else if he had gone back without a race,' said the trainer, who changed his mind, not without considerable misgivings.

As he watched Billy Ellison lead Red Rum round the parade ring, he looked closely at Red Rum and must have felt immense pride in the horse's condition. He was a bundle of muscle and much the most imposing individual of the seven. Sandra Kendall believed he hated the rain and was a different horse when the sun shone. Certainly, he didn't show any of his characteristic exuberance in the paddock that day. Inevitably by then, he had top weight. On this occasion 12 st. 7 lb. Tregarron, though to have thrown off the effects of the cough, had 27 lb. less and Fanatic, a useful-looking young chaser trained by Neville Crump and ridden by Pat Buckley, carried only 10 st.

As Donald McCain gave Brian a leg up, Brian told him; 'Well, Don, I'm going out here with the National in the back of my mind and on no account am I going to give this horse a hard race. I'm going to nurse him round. And if the worst comes to the worst I'm going to pull him up!' The trainer, of course, agreed with his plan of action and walked away to the stands content that if the ground was too deep for Red Rum at least he would not be needlessly persevered with.

Brian did not hurry Red Rum while Saggart's Choice, sadly a shadow of his former self, led for the first two miles. As they set out on the final circuit he moved him up closer to Fanatic, who had taken the lead, and he delivered his challenged turning for home. He was alongside Fanatic at the last, where Fanatic made a wholesale blunder and virtually came to a standstill, though Pet Buckley miraculously stayed aboard and Fanatic kept his feet.

'I was pleased to see Pat make a mistake on Fanatic, because that made things much easier for Red Rum, and I did not even have to slap him down the neck. But Red Rum would have won in any case,' Brian states. His winning distance was eight lengths. The third horse, also receiving two and a half stone, was twelve lengths further back. Donald McCain was relieved and thrilled by Red Rum's victory. And he had yet another quote to please the racing correspondents; 'He will win the Grand National, given our ground.' Ground, that is, which was no worse than good.

The Greenall Whitley at Haydock on March 2 was again to be Red Rum's last race before Aintree. Of those who had opposed him in the race in the previous season, Money Market and Tregarron were entered again. Money Market, despite a twelve-length win at Sandown, was to receive 26 lb. from Red Rum and Tregarron 27 lb. compared with 13 lb. and 10 lb. respectively in the 1973 event. Tregarron was preferred to Red Rum in the betting and favourite was the novice discovery of the season, Glanford Brigg, a dashing front-runner.

Glanford Brigg set off in the lead and jumped the first fence well. Red Rum jumped it brilliantly, passing two horses in the air, but as he landed he was knocked sideways by the swerving Noble Hero. Brian was bowled out of the saddle and with him, so it seemed, went Donald McCain's carefully-laid strategy leading to Liverpool.

'I was a bit upset when I saw Brian up his neck,' Donald recalls. 'But once Red Rum had decided to race with the others even without a jockey I had no qualms at all. He thoroughly enjoyed himself and the race was just what he needed.' He made his way down from the stands to the centre of the course and watched the race with Alan Mactaggart, the amateur jockey, trainer and steward. 'I had a level bet with him that Red Rum would win riderless,' he adds. And he came near to collecting.

Red Rum jumped round with Glanford Brigg, who was well clear of the others still in the race. Donald takes up the story. 'He was with Glanford Brigg when Glanford Brigg went up the shoot on the inside of the open ditch which is jumped twice but not on the last circuit. Red Rum looked towards Glanford Brigg and you could see his brain ticking. His ears went backwards and forwards and then he said, "No, that's wrong." He was quite emphatic about it. He straightened up and jumped the open ditch and the water and said, "Now, that's the way you should go." He was teaching a novice his job.'

Red Rum then pulled himself up and Donald had no difficulty in catching him. Back at his stable he fed him with a bucket and a half of mash. 'He ate every bit. While I suppose we are sorry to have missed such a valuable prize, I think it was better for him to have the race without a jockey on his back than it would have been for him to go round with 12 st. 7 lb. And he didn't have a mark on him; he had cleared every fence with a bit to spare,' Donald McCain said the next day.

If any incident gives a clue to the reason for the trainer's extraordinary success it is this one : he treats his horses as individuals and the responsibility attached to training them is something which he relishes. Worry, to him, is pointless. Making the best of a situation is his policy.

As Grand National day, March 30, drew nearer the weather began to improve. The snow of Cheltenham Monday amazingly dispersed and the Festival meeting went ahead and showed, among other things, that L'Escargot would be a danger to Red Rum in the Grand National by dividing Soothsayer, a new Fred Winter star, and Clever Scot in the Cathcart Challenge Cup. Spanish Steps gave his National prospects a fillip by running second in the National Hunt Handicap Chase and Royal Relief recaptured the Two-Mile Champion Chase title. Rough House also ran a first-rate National trial in the Kim Muir Memorial Cup, staying on strongly in the last three-quarters of a mile to take third place to Castleruddery.

Donald McCain had been taken aback at first when told that Red Rum had been allotted top weight of 12 st. in the National in the absence of Crisp, sadly a casualty since their Doncaster meeting. But he had stated previously that he would fancy Red Rum to beat L'Escargot at level weights and, on reflection, he was satisfied that the handicapper had done a fair job. Red Rum was one pound above L'Escargot, 5 lb. above Spanish Steps and two stone above Arthur Stephenson's Scout, who was to be ridden by Tommy Stack, now retained by the Bishop Auckland stable.

CHAPTER SIXTEEN

Red Rum's training at home closely followed the schedule of the 1972–73 season. He continued to thrive and on the eve of the Grand National he was taken to the sands for his final workout. 'I worked him over five and half furlongs very sharply, and then sent him back and he worked over four furlongs. This had wound him up a little bit and when Billy started to pull him up I thought there would be no need to take him to Liverpool the next day – he would get there himself. He disappeared in the right direction with Billy swinging off him and shouting and seething and doing everything he shouldn't do. I thought, "Well, I'll just pick him up when I get there." But that is Red Rum, a great character,' Donald McCain related later.

The routine on National day was as before and by mid-morning Red Rum was safely installed in his box at Aintree. So were Glenkiln and The Tunku, making a trio of McCain runners. Red Rum had been a clear favourite in the advance betting and the *Sporting Life* forecast betting on the big day gave him as 8 to 1 favourite. L'Escargot was at 10 to 1, Straight Vulgan at fourteens and Scout at sixteens, along with Franco-phile, Rough House and Sunny Lad. Ladbroke's and Joe Coral had Red Rum at 7 to 1 and Mecca at 13 to 2.

Thirteen of the twenty-one racing correspondents whose nap selections are given every day in the *Sporting Life* had chosen the Grand National and of these Scotia (*Scottish Daily Express*), the Scout (*Daily Express*) and The Duke (*Yorkshire Post*) had napped Red Rum. Straight Vulgan was the *Sporting Life*'s form selection, though he had been unimpressive in his last race,

116

Kettledrum, of the *Sporting Chronicle,* was one of two opting for Royal Relief, to be ridden by Lord Oaksey.

Hot sunshine had dried out the going, so that after being 'good' on Topham Trophy day it was firm on the Friday and firmer still on the Saturday, which dawned clear and bright. Early arrivals at the course were able to view the fences in sunshine which would have graced a June day. Donald McCain had the ground he wanted for Red Rum and his confidence was unbounded.

No horse since Reynoldstown in 1935 and 1936 had won the National in successive years. Reynoldstown had risen 12 lb. in the weights in 1936 and was a very fortunate winner for Davy Jones ran out at the last fence when holding a clear lead. No horse had successfully defied such a steep rise in the handicap between Grand Nationals as that imposed Red Rum, and since 1843, when the race became a handicap, only seven winners had carried 12 st. or more. Reynoldstown was the last of them.

As number one on the racecard, Red Rum led the parade on to the course. From the Press stand, high above the winning post, he seemed keen – even slightly on edge. Keen? – 'Yes,' said Brian later. 'Excited, too. You would have thought it was his first race of the season not his ninth.' Princess Camilla, in new ownership, showed signs of over-excitement again but more eyes were on Red Rum and Scout. Astonishingly, Scout's price had tumbled from 18 to 1 to less than half price and he started favourite at 7 to 1. Red Rum drifted out to elevens as L'Escargot closed in to 17 to 2.

Brian edged across to his favourite position, towards the outside, as the last of the numbers were called by the starter. Down went the flag and away went the forty-two runners in the 130th Grand National. Red Rum jumped off smartly. 'Going into the first few fences, I was having difficulty in restraining him,' says Brian. Royal Relief was the only casualty at the first, Sixer went at the fourth, and six left the race at the Canal Turn. Red Rum kept out of trouble on his outside path as Sunny Lad and Charles Dickens led the field back towards the stands followed by Pearl of Montreal Straight Vulgan and Vulgan Town.

Brian picked up the Sunny Lad colours and kept them in sight. He was a good jumper and one to bear in mind when they reached the Chair. 'It is such a dicey fence to jump. I went down there the day before the race and thought, "What the hell, this fence looks bigger than ever." I wanted a good lead into to it so that I wouldn't be bothered by loose horses or falling horses. All this went through my mind on that first circuit as I concentrated on getting a clear round.'

The pace was much steadier than when Crisp was there to set it and both L'Escargot and Spanish Steps had been able to lie up with the leaders. Vulgan Town and Pearl of Montreal led over the water, with Charles Dickens and Sunny Lad. Red Rum was well placed just behind them and nothing was going better than Scout. Straight Vulgan fell at the second fence on the run towards Becher's and Glenkiln at the following ditch.

Charles Dickens, his breastplate broken and his saddle starting to slip back, led on the run towards Becher's but did not get there first. Red Rum had that distinction. 'I did not want to fight him and waste his energy by restraining him so I let him bowl along and he hit the front at Becher's second time.' Brian adds. He already had noted one possible danger 'L'Escargot was on the inside going down the back second time, when I was fourth or fifth. L'Escargot was running away and I thought that the way he was holding his position this time he would be the danger.'

'Red Rum is a lazy horse when in front on his own and my big worry after Becher's was that if L'Escargot could sit in behind me he might have the foot to beat me.' The Irish horse, meeting Red Rum on 24 lb. better terms than in the 1973 National, moved past Charles Dickens and into second place before the Canal Turn and narrowed the gap between himself and Red Rum ominously when Red Rum made his first Aintree mistake.

'He really rooted the last ditch, the fourth from home, and for a moment I thought he would lose his legs on landing. But he recovered quickly and I knew before the second last that he had the beating of L'Escargot,' Brian states. He knew that he had the beating of everything else, too, for Red Rum still was galloping strongly and, that blemish behind him, his jumping was back to normal. Had there been a Crisp out in front it seemed he could have sprinted up the run-in with his 12 st. just as effectively as he had with 10 st. 5 lb.

His lead over L'Escargot, some four lengths at the last, doubled in another hundred and fifty yards. Charles Dickens was running on again but was too far behind to have any chance of victory. Then, not far from the point where Devon Loch's imminent victory became disaster eighteen years earlier, Brian stood high in his stirrups and waved to the crowd. 'After a horse and rider have gone four and a half miles anyone was entitled to think, "What the hell is he doing," but I was overcome with joy, excitement, emotion and instinctively I saluted the crowd.'

The waving over, he settled back to ride Red Rum stylishly past the post a long-looking seven lengths ahead of Charles Dickens who caught L'Escargot in the final stride. Jackie Grainger, Donald McCain's head lad, was waiting at the side of the course and so Red Rum's second triumphant return to the winner's enclosure began. This time the cheering was all for him, unquestionably now one of the best Grand National winners of all time and worthy to rank with the legendary Golden Miller. Although the pace on the first circuit had been moderate and although Red Rum was eased in the last hundred yards, his time of nine minutes twenty and a half seconds was only one tenth of a second slower than that of Golden Miller in 1934 and that had stood as a record until Red Rum's battle with Crisp. Of course, some of the fences had been modified and the take-off side sloped but the open ditches are still as they were in Golden Miller's day.

At the ensuing Press conference, Brian took the questions first again. He paid tribute to Donald McCain for 'the wonderful job he has done with the horse' and to Red Rum, 'He is such a great horse, anyone could have won the National on him.' What had been his feelings at Becher's? 'Had I hit the front too soon? But I knew he would keep going and would jump' . . . 'The mistake at the ditch was his only one throughout' . . . 'When I saw television on Thursday and learned that the ground was good I knew that if he had a good run round he would take all the beating.'

The racing correspondents all knew by now that Donald McCain was an engaging talker and frank one, so he did not escape as lightly as he had done the previous spring. 'I always was pretty sure about the outcome but when you look back you think, "Who the hell do you think you are; you aren't going to carry 12 st. around Liverpool. You can sit on you bum and talk about it but he has got to go out and do it." What I wanted this victory for was for the horse's sake, because we all sit here and talk but this horse has made himself into what he is. Seven years to the day, Grand National-wise, this horse dead-heated in a seller here. What he has become since then he has become in spite of human beings not because of them. That's my opinion,' said an emotional Donald McCain.

One correspondent prefaced his question with, 'You have improved the horse so much between . . .' He did not get any further. 'I haven't improved him, he has improved himself,' declared Donald. 'He has just been waiting for his opportunity, he has got it and he has taken it. He has done everything he has had to do, with Brian's assistance. They have developed the most wonderful partnership.'

The author could not refrain from asking the obvious. 'Are you looking forward to next year.' And the trainer could not keep back his optimism. 'Yes, I am. I hope it doesn't sound too cocky, but he can win it again next year, given the ground.'

'Keep quiet, don't tell anybody,' interjected Brian.

Had he had any anxiety with Red Rum? 'This horse doesn't give you any anxiety, except that you might be doing too much with him. The blacksmith came in at the beginning of the week and said, "This fellow has put on half a hundred-weight, since I last saw him." Straight away you think, "Oh Lord, what have I done wrong." If he had come in and said he had lost half a hundredweight I would still have had those doubts. He is a super blacksmith but he worries me to death.'

What about the rest of the season? 'I'll have to see how he is when I get home. He is in the Scottish Grand National and the Whitbread. The Dikler is set to give him a stone at Ayr. The weights aren't out for the Whitbread, but I would think that any intelligent handicapper would set him to give a stone to The Dikler,' said the trainer with a broad smile. 'I will discuss this with Mr le Mare – because he is rather hard up at the moment!' Then, more seriously. 'This is horse we have had tremendous pleasure out of and I would like to think that this is his last race this season. We have come to Liverpool and he has done his job. But we will talk about it.'

Hadn't he had the French National in mind? 'Yes. But he would have had to have anti-flu injections and, whatever the steward say, I think it is a silly idea. All the horses of mine which have had the injections have been sick horses afterwards. This fellow is not going to have any needles stuck in him, at any price.'

Back at Southport, Red Rum gave every sign that the National had not been any more arduous a race than any of the others he had contested. He ate well, he was full of bounce and high spirits, and he looked as well as ever. And he was to make Donald McCain change his mind about the Scottish Grand National.

CHAPTER SEVENTEEN

Brian Fletcher had hoped that the trainer would adhere to his first thoughts about the Scottish Grand National and give it a miss. Uppermost in his mind was his recollection of Red Alligator in the year of his Grand National victory. 'He went to complete the great double, and at Ayr he was a dead horse; he just did not want to know. In fact, he was never the same horse again. I was thinking it would be an awful shame for a horse who had won two Grand Nationals to come out in a four-mile chase at Ayr and for people to see the worst side of him.'

Donald McCain was confident that Red Rum would be an exception to that 'never-the-same-horse-again' theory. Hadn't he already shown that by making such improvement since his first Grand National win? Though the Scottish National would be his tenth race of the season, he had been given his mid-season rest. So, Red Rum made the journey to Ayr on Friday April 19. The next day he was to carry 11 st. 13 lb., for the weights had been raised in the absence of The Dikler and Red Rum had a 6 lb. penalty for his Aintree victory. One of the two other penalised horses in the race was Proud Tarquin, and even with his penalty for a smooth win at Doncaster he would be receiving 20 lb. from Red Rum. In the Grand National of 1973, Proud Tarquin had been assessed at 6 lb. superior to Donald McCain's horse.

Scout was in opposition again, as was Deblin's Green and Francophile. The latter, thought to be destined for better things than Red Rum early in their careers, had won five times that season for Reg Lamb, a capable trainer at Seahouses in Northumberland. He had then been sold before the Grand National for a five-figure sum though Reg Lamb's early impression had been that he was not big enough for the Liverpool fences. He had gone on to refuse at Liverpool, projecting Richard Pitman into riderless flight.

One of the biggest Ayr crowds of all time turned out to see Red Rum and most of them placed their bets on him, causing his price to be cut to 11 to 8. They had more confidence than Brian, though he was greatly impressed by Red Rum's appearance in the paddock. 'He looked tremendously well.'

Down at the start, Pat Buckley looked over his shoulder on Canharis and told Brian, 'that horse does look well, Brian.'

'He does look very well, Pat,' Brian replied, 'But believe me he has not given me the same feeling cantering down to the post, even walking round here, that he did at Liverpool.' At Liverpool, Brian had been thrilled to find him on his toes. He was apprehensive now.

That apprehension was for the horse, not for himself. 'All I was concerned with in the race was to nurse him as long as I possibly could. I had no intention of letting him down and giving him a hard race. If Red Rum was feeling his Aintree race I wasn't going to bother at all. I wanted to give him every confidence in jumping the low fences again – if he had gone out and spent too much time in the air thinking he was going round Liverpool again, that would have cost him the race. I was determined to look after him, to give him every chance. If it had come to the crunch and he hadn't been well enough to keep him in a good position, I would have pulled him up. This was understood with Don McCain.'

Canharis, taken out of the National, had won well at Newcastle early in the month and he continued in the same vein, setting a strong pace and surviving two comprehensive blunders. Lord Oaksey took Proud Tarquin ahead at the eighteenth fence and established a clear lead. Thoughts of victory were beginning to form when, three fences from home, he glanced right and saw Red Rum's head inching nearer.

'Red Rum, though never giving me the same feel that he had at Liverpool, had the class to hold his position and I was able to nurse him along and take him up to Proud Tarquin. I was worried when he hit the second last, the last ditch, and it took

him a bit of time to get into his stride again. I gave him a
slap approaching the last, he met it dead right, pinged it and
sprinted away. I was very surprised,' Brian states.

In the first 30 yards after the fence, his acceleration sank
all Lord Oaksey's hopes and Red Rum won comfortably in the
end by four lengths to the accompaniment of the loudest cheering ever heard at Ayr. The first prize of £7,922 brought his
winnings for the season to almost £37,000, breaking his
National Hunt record of the previous season when he won
£28,883. A further prize of £12,500 awaited him the following
Saturday at Sandown, in the Whitbread Gold Cup, but Donald
McCain and Mr le Mare resisted the temptation.

'I am getting on to Weatherby's right now so we can't be
tempted to run him,' Donald McCain told the Press the next
day. 'We have been sorely tempted but we feel the horse has
done enough. He went straight to his manger when he got
back from Ayr and he is as bright as a cricket, but if he
travelled to Sandown and didn't win, it wouldn't be the horse
who got beat, it would be us who got him beat by being too
ambitious.'

Brian thought he might have won the Whitbread, an impression confirmed when Proud Tarquin finished a head in front
of The Dikler carrying 8 lb. overweight, only to lose the race
in the stewards' room, but he was very glad that the trainer
had left him at Southport. All that remained for Red Rum now
was to be eased off again in readiness for a long summer at
grass, sharing his paddock with a donkey.

He was nine years old, his legs were as sound as they were
when he made his racing debut seven years earlier and physically he was in his prime. Donald McCain reasoned that he
should still be at his peak the next season and his campaign for
the 1974–75 season was to be planned on the same lines as in
the two preceding ones. He believed that a third Grand
National could be Red Rum's, provided only that the weather
was kind and the ground reasonably fast.

Brian Fletcher preferred not to project his thoughts so far
ahead. 'There is a tendency to talk about the National and
Red Rum as though it is like going down the road and then
coming back. But when it gets to those last few minutes before
the off, all the responsibility is with the jockey. One mistake and

all the plans can be ruined. It's a great race – the world's finest steeplechase – but it's nice to get it over with and settle down to a medium sort of life again. Once the year turns, it will be soon enough for me to look forward to Liverpool and to riding the horse with the biggest heart I have ever known there again.'

It is not certain, of course, that Red Rum will run in a third Grand National, even if his training goes exactly to plan. There were several 'last' Grand Nationals in the days that Mrs Mirabel Topham's company had absolute control. One has the feeling that Mr Bill Davies, to whom Mrs Topham sold the Aintree course for £3m., would have just one 'last' National should he decide to end racing there.

The £3m. deal was announced, with many smiles and kisses all round, before the 1974 Grand National meeting. Mr Davies, it was stated, had undertaken to continue the National for at least five years and his aim was to bring back a full racing programme to Aintree and to revive motor racing on the track built by Mrs Topham. He began his reign by negotiating new television rights with overseas countries and by selling advertising space round the inside of the parade ring and on 'the biggest advertising hoarding in the world,' situated on the bank on the run towards Becher's. These were the moves of a sensible and alert business man, aware of the revenue potential of a world-famous event which created interest in virtually every country in the world. He forecast advertisement revenue of £½m. in 1975.

He bumped up the fees paid by bookmakers, so that a cheap-enclosure bookmaker with a staff of two would have to pay £12 compared with £1.50 in the Topham days. And he introduced stiff increases in entrance and parking fees for the public. A meeting with bookmakers' representatives resulted in some cuts in the proposed charges but the public found their admittance fees high – some prohibitive, so that they turned their cars round and blocked the streets round the course.

Mr. Davies appeared before the Press, at a conference organised by the Racing Information Bureau, on Grand National day. It was, in some respects, a sad occasion and, certainly, a disturbing one. Mr Davies did not mind discouraging the public from bringing their cars to Aintree, he said, because he preferred them to park their cars well away from the course and use public transport.

Whether or not the B.B.C. were going to be allowed to televise the National again depended on the verdict of one of his employees who had spent the day watching the B.B.C. coverage. His task had been to see whether the cameras dwelt long enough on the advertisements on the course or whether they had given Mr Davies's advertisers a 'raw deal'. The fact that the B.B.C. Charter does not permit cameramen to dwell on advertisements seemed of little moment to Mr Davies. If his man's report showed that the B.B.C. had not done the job to his satisfaction, then the B.B.C. would not get a renewed contract to televise the National; there was no question of I.T.V. having a contract.

Well, if there was to be no television what would happen to his advertisers? There was no satisfactory answer to that one from Mr Davies, the local lad who made good and is the head of the Walton property group. He had grandiose plans for Aintree; it would become a great centre of racing once more – and not just one one day of the year. He would tour the world's racecourses and incorporate the best of their ideas in the revaulised Aintree. All this subject, however, to his obtaining planning permission for a huge shopping supermarket on part of Aintree.

The ifs and buts were of a magnitude which made those with a serious concern for the future of Aintree racecourse and the Grand National in particular feel considerable unease. Racing needs its great events if it is to prosper and the Grand National, with the Derby, are the twin pillars of racing popularity in Britain. Whether or not Mr Davies and his company need the Grand National remains to be seen.

He organised the 1974 Grand National meeting without investing any money over and above that always invested in the meeting by the Topham private company. The stands were in their usual state of rudimentary functionalism and the litter roamed freely. When he has to pay the money needed to give the National the setting it deserves, will the revenue satisfy him? On such a slender thread does the future of Aintree hang. Racing's administrators should be castigated for allowing such a situation to arise.

If Red Rum is denied an attempt at the Grand National

hat-trick, he will be diverted instead to the Cheltenham Gold Cup. Tommy Stack, who knows him so well, believes that he could win a Gold Cup – indeed, that he could have won the 1974 Gold Cup. Brian Fletcher has his doubts, but sees it as an academic argument. 'Red Rum is a great Aintree horse, maybe the greatest of all time. I'm privileged to have been associated with him.'

INDEX

Edwards, Roy, 39, 40-1; Fletcher, Brian, 86, 87, 90, 109-10, 111, 112-13, 113-14, 122-4; Gifford, Josh, 28; Gifford, Macer, 47, 57; Gillam, Andy, 52; Grand National, 95-104, 116-19; Haydock Park, 85, 91, 92, 113-14; Kelso, 52; Leicester, 16; McCain, Donald, 61-2, 86; Market Rasen, 29-30; Newbury, 111; Newcastle, 43-4, 52, 84; Nottingham, 57; Oxclose, 27-8, 42-3; Perth, 41, 108; Piggott, Lester, 22; Renton, Robert, 24ff; Sandown, 49; Stack, Tommy, 36, 37-8, 40-1, 43-4, 45, 51, 55-6, 58, 60, 82-3, 84, 85; Teesside Park, 32-4, 39, 49, 50; Turnell, Andy, 29-30; Wetherby, 39, 41-2, 47, 74

Red Sweeney, 52, 53, 60, 92

Rouge Autumn, 94, 100, 101, 102, 104

Royal Relief, 92, 93, 110, 117

Scout, 115, 116, 117, 122

Slave's Dream, 52, 59, 87

Soloning, 29, 30, 40, 45, 46

Spanish Steps, 94, 95, 96, 102, 104, 115, 118

Straight Vulcan, 92, 94, 109, 116, 117

Sunny Lad, 78, 79, 87, 110, 116, 117, 118

Supermaster, 39, 46, 50, 57, 58, 83

Tartuffe, 68-9

Tregarron, 84, 92, 93, 109, 112, 113

Walshaw Demon, 70-2

War Cry, 72

Young Ash Leaf, 18, 57, 58, 60

JOCKEYS

Barry, Ron, 33, 73, 82, 83, 84, 87, 88, 90, 94, 99, 109

Biddlecombe, Terry, 10, 11, 13, 38

Blackshaw, Martin, 59

Broderick, Paddy, 13, 29, 30-4, 37, 43-4, 56, 59

Brogan, Barry, 39

Buckley, Pat, 10, 13, 113, 123

Doyle, John, 30, 36; Tony, 30, 46

Edwards, Ray, 13, 39, 40

Enright, John, 53, 54, 58, 84, 90

Fletcher, Brian, 8-15, 23, 33, 57, 64, 84, 88, 97, 99, 104, 106, 120, 127; Ayr, 48, 67, 72, 73, 87, 122-4; Caleys Harvest, 72; Canharis, 73-4; Carlisle, 90, 109-10; Catterick, 112-13; Cheltenham, 19, 27, 31; Clever Scot, 31; Corseal, 48, Dickinson, Tony, 89; Dondieu, 39, 67; Flapping, 9; Grand National, 8, 20-1, 65-6, 96, 100-4, 117-19; Haydock Park, 17, 113-14; Hexham, 17; Kelso, 52; Newbury, 111; Newcastle, 52, 73-4; Red Alligator, 11-15, 20-1, 65-6; Red Rum, 18, 86, 87, 109-10, 112-13, 117-19; Sedgefield, 72; Slave's Dream, 52; Smith, Denys, 9-10; Tartuffe, 69; Teesside Park, 68, 72; Walshaw Demon, 72; War Cry, 72; Wetherby, 39, 73; Wilkinson, Jumbo, 91

Gifford, Josh, 11, 27, 28, 29, 99

Gifford, Macer, 48, 57, 58

King, Jeff, 94, 99

Mellor, Stan, 13, 31, 47, 48, 58

Mould, David, 19, 99

Nicholson, David, 54, 99

Oaksley, *Lord*, 97, 102, 117, 123

O'Neill, Jonjo, 90, 98

Piggott, Lester, 7, 22, 28

Pitman, Richard, 93, 99, 100, 103, 104, 105, 106, 123

Stack, Tommy, 27, 32, 35-6, 37, 38, 40, 41, 42, 43, 45, 47-8, 50, 51-4, 55, 57, 58, 60, 73, 81, 82, 83, 84, 85, 94, 115, 126

RACES AND MEETINGS

Aintree, Liverpool, 10, 11, 38, 44, 76, 125, 126; BP Shield Handicap Hurdle, 96; Earl of Sefton

130